MAKING **TOYS**
THAT **TEACH**

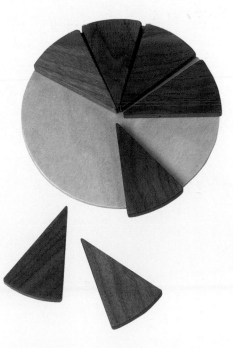

MAKING TOYS THAT TEACH

with

Step-by-Step Instructions and Plans

Les Neufeld

The Taunton Press

The Taunton Press
Inspiration for hands-on living®

The Taunton Press, Inc., 63 South Main Street, PO Box 5506,
Newtown, CT 06470-5506
e-mail: tp@taunton.com

Editor: Stefanie Ramp
Jacket/Cover design: Mary McKeon
Interior design: Carol Petro
Layout: Carol Petro
Illustrator: Melanie Powell
Photographers: Les Neufeld and Scott Phillips

Library of Congress Cataloging-in-Publication Data
Neufeld, Les.
  Making toys that teach : with step-by-step instructions and plans /
Les Neufeld.
       p. cm.
Includes bibliographical references.
  ISBN-13: 978-1-56158-606-6
  ISBN-10: 1-56158-606-4
  1. Wooden toy making. 2. Educational toys. I. Title.
  TT174.5.W6 N48 2003
  745.592--dc21

                                2003001363

Printed in the United States of America
10 9 8 7 6 5 4 3

The following brand names/manufacturers are trademarked: Amana Tool®,
Bridgewood®, CMT®, Delta®, DeWalt®, Felder®, Freud®, General®, Gudho®,
Grizzly®, Incra®, Jet Equipment & Tools®, Makita®, Porter Cable®,
Powermatic®, Q-tip®, Ridgid®, Ryobi®, Shopsmith®, and Tried & True®.

Working with wood is inherently dangerous. Using hand or power tools improp-
erly or ignoring safety practices can lead to permanent injury or even death.
Don't try to perform operations you learn about here (or elsewhere) unless
you're certain they are safe for you. If something about an operation doesn't
feel right, don't do it. Look for another way. We want you to enjoy the craft,
so please keep safety foremost in your mind whenever you're in the shop.

To my father, Elvin Neufeld,
a fine parent, educator, and craftsman

acknowledgments

My children have often spurred me on to design, build, and improve
a great variety of wooden toys and so deserve credit for these toys being
more useful than they might otherwise have been. Thank you Eric,
Kevin, and Lisa.

Corrinne, I thank you for your constant support. You have been wonderful.

There are several fellow educators whom I can always count on for help,
advice, and ideas. Thank you Tony, Dave, Mark, Laurie, and Dennis.

For their support, I thank the various members of my immediate and
extended family. Although I hesitate to single out one person, I must give
a special thanks to Roger for his continual interest and encouragement.

Tom Clark was instrumental in developing the original concept
for this book. Jenny Peters did a lot of the initial running around and
communicating. Thank you both. Stefanie Ramp did a great job
of editing and improving the manuscript in countless ways. Your work
was very much appreciated. Thank you, Stef.

Others at Taunton worked on editing, design, photography, and layout.
It is a wonderful thing to hand off a rather crude-looking manuscript
and have it come out as an attractive book. Thank you all.

contents

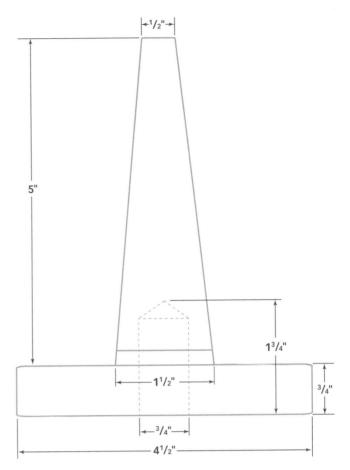

introduction

*f*ew experiences have had as profound an impact on my life as having children. Eric, the first of our three, was a great child and is now a fine young man, though he always did walk to the beat of his own drum. As a toddler, his complete disregard for conventional toys was a great surprise, and although I tried a great variety of shiny, noisy toys, Eric preferred to play with the boxes they came in. I have found out since that, to some extent, many parents have had similar experiences.

There were times when Eric, as a toddler, was bored and would amble about not doing much of anything. I was in the middle of working on a master's degree in education and was all too aware of current research regarding the importance of stimulation and activity for young children's development. As a young parent, I neared panic level and started to make toys that would be more likely to interest and challenge Eric. By the time our third child came around, I must confess that I was no longer as intense, but my concern did serve to influence me to start making toys.

Some toys did not pass Eric's standards for interest, and others did not pass the test of time and durability, as they passed through the hands of two more children (Kevin and Lisa). However, some toys endured, and they show up in this book with slight modifications. A few come as ideas from other parents and educators and a few have been traditional favorites for hundreds of years.

Many of the most successful toys are the simplest. My father presented Eric with a simple set of wooden blocks in various shapes and made from a variety of woods. Most were cut from scraps gathered from his shop floor. My kids played with these for years. Later a friend made a set of oversize pine domino blocks, and I was often called by Kevin and Lisa to "come look" at their many strange and wonderful uses for these dominoes. The shape puzzle box is an exact copy of the first development toy I made for Eric (during a parental panic)—the only toy that endured unmodified and undamaged to this day, despite much use.

Make the toys as carefully as your personality dictates. Durability is important, but the educational value does not diminish with a few sanding scratches left in or with a train car that is ⅛ in. too short. Your satisfaction may be affected, however, so the craftsmanship required in these projects is up to you. I think the toy should start out as flawless as you are prepared to make it, but keep in mind that these are toys to be used in young hands.

Children will dent and scratch them eventually, so it is a different level of long-term care than might be appropriate with a beautiful china cabinet.

No project part uses a large amount of wood or takes a large amount of time. Don't let it worry you if some mistakes are made along the way; you have wasted little time or money and have gained experience. I have heard it said that experience is what you get when you didn't get what you wanted to get. That is probably true, but in woodworking, experience is a valuable asset all the same.

I not only enjoy making these projects for those reasons but also because of the pleasure I see on my children's faces as they receive and play with the toys. I don't wonder if the toy is too loud, junky, or somehow detrimental to the child's development. These toys are just the opposite.

Build these toys knowing that your handmade toys are those most likely to be around for more than one generation and that have a value attached to them that is far above the actual monetary figure.

Making Toys That Teach

all parents want toys that nurture and develop the creativity and learning ability that children naturally possess. These toys should be fun, but they should also be educational tools that allow us to give children opportunities to grow. As a parent, educator, and woodworker, I had a natural desire to create such toys.

I also wanted to encourage beginning woodworkers to tackle toy making. To that end I have attempted to keep the projects in this book free of any roadblocks that might hinder a person who is not highly skilled or does not have expensive machinery—no complex inlays or hand-cut joints here. And accordingly, the shop equipment and space required has been kept modest.

It is my hope that beginning woodworkers not only tackle the projects but enjoy them as well; hobbies that cause frustration are rarely pursued, and woodworking is definitely worth pursuing. The layout of the book is organized in such a way as to ensure clarity and to answer as many questions as possible along the way.

Layout of the Book

After nearly 25 years of teaching apprentices, teenagers, and novice adults, I am a firm believer in pictures and drawings as a means of simplifying communication. Wherever possible, photos accompany the written instructions. If you glance through a chapter looking only at the photos and drawings, you should have a pretty good idea of how to build the project. The text is there to fill in any gaps and restate what is being demonstrated in a photo in case there is a question about the technical details.

because some key piece of equipment is unavailable. If you know ahead of time that you need a ⁹⁄₁₆-in. drill bit, you can likely beg, borrow, or steal one for a day or two. If nothing else, it will give you an excuse to go to the local tool-supply store and make another purchase. For more specific information on tools and buying tips, see p. 10.

In the introduction to each project, you will find a comment about the time involved. This will vary depending on the experience and personality of the reader and to some extent on the equipment available. However, the estimate will give you a decent approximation of the time each project requires.

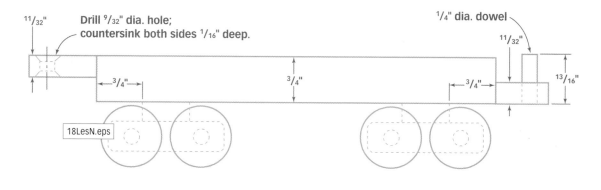

Drill ⁹⁄₃₂" dia. hole; countersink both sides ¹⁄₁₆" deep. — ¹¹⁄₃₂" — ¼" dia. dowel — ¹¹⁄₃₂" — ¾" — ¾" — ¾" — ¾" — ¹³⁄₁₆" — 18LesN.eps

Drawings, or "blueprints," are a necessity. Although all the sizes appear on the drawings, I have often restated the dimensions in the text as a means of ensuring clarity. In many places, I have ignored strict drafting dimension conventions in order to make the drawings clearer. For instance, a given dimension may be repeated on a top view and a side view of a project.

Each project also has a cut list. While you could gather this information from the drawings, it is always nicer to have the list in front of you as you start. In some more involved projects, such as the Ultimate Building Block Set, an idea of the total amount of wood required has also been included at the beginning of the chapter.

At the beginning of each chapter, you will also find a list of tools you'll need. This is included to prevent you from reaching some point in a project when you realize you cannot reasonably continue

The projects themselves are organized from the least complex and time-consuming to the most complex. The first chapters have projects that require minimal experience and skills, while the latter projects are more elaborate, although still within the ability of any patient and careful woodworker. I have assumed that any chapter is the place you may start, so there is some repetition from toy to toy where procedures are similar. In a few cases, the instructions refer you to another chapter where that particular procedure has already been outlined in detail.

A sidebar at the end of each chapter called "Learning through Play" will give you a quick overview of the educational value of each toy. A variety of suggestions are included regarding play and educational opportunities—playtime can become more enjoyable and valuable when it is guided now and then. These suggestions are intended to help point a child in useful directions and maximize the educational benefit of each toy. I am hoping that as you read these suggestions many more ideas will spring to mind, and combined with the child's imagination, you should have a treasure trove of possibilities.

At the start of each "Learning though Play" sidebar, you will also find a note about the approximate age level for each toy. Most toys have a broad range of ages because they can be used one way when a child is very young and in different ways as time passes. I have often given toys to my own children that were too advanced for them, and it took a year or two before they could make good use of them. In my experience it is best to let young children have fun with the simpler toys and not force more complicated play on them until they are developmentally ready—an age that tends to be different for every child.

Teaching through Play

The "Learning through Play" sidebar suggests different kinds of play that have various educational goals attached. It is helpful to have a basic understanding of how each type is used by educators, so you'll be better able to guide your child.

Convergent vs. Divergent Play

Many toys have predetermined and quite limited types of use—coloring books or wind-up toys, for example. With these toys, there is really only one possible outcome in play, which is called convergent play. Other toys have many outcomes, limited only by imagination; this is divergent play. For most educational and developmental goals, divergent (or open-ended) play is preferable. All the toys in this book provide opportunity for divergent play.

Fostering Creativity

Years ago, when I was young and my son Eric was even younger, he started to play and make things in my shop. At first, I thought this was great, but it didn't take long until my limited patience was taxed. He made mistakes. He didn't set my precious tools down the way I thought they should be set down. He sometimes left a mess or spilled some finish. Fortunately, I soon realized that this was the price of encouraging his interest and his creativity. If it cost me a tool or some spilled finish, fine.

Creativity naturally exists in children, but to encourage it means allowing some room for error and mess; we all learn through mistakes and messes of various sorts. To put down strict limits on play teaches that creativity has little or negative value.

Sometimes parents discourage creativity without even realizing it. A number of educators (see Further Reading on p. 135) have found that straight praise can actually discourage creativity in children because they will repeat whatever they have done in hopes of being praised again. When a child creates something with blocks, for instance, discuss the details of what they've made and how and why they made it that way, rather than merely complimenting them. Then encourage them to create something totally different.

It is my hope that the toys in this book, and the play that goes with them, will provide many chances for creativity to grow. With each toy, allow and encourage children to be creative to see what they can invent and discover.

Problem Solving

Increasing emphasis has been placed on problem solving in recent years, and with good reason. Memorizing an outcome is fine, but being able to work through a problem and reach a logical outcome is a more versatile strategy. Problem solving goes hand in hand with creativity because with open-ended play comes a variety of problems. For example, stacking large blocks on smaller ones creates a tower that will topple quickly. Why? How can it be built higher?

There are different strategies that can be used to work through problems, and these toys will provide many opportunities to talk with kids about problem-solving techniques. The educational value is taken a step further if you talk to a child about simple ways to tackle problems in general, not just the one that has arisen through play. What exactly

Research on Educational *Toys*

WHILE COMMON SENSE tells us that children benefit from educational, interactive play and that it is all too often ignored in favor of television and video games, a number of studies have proven the point in recent years. While an exhaustive study of all academic research would belabor the point, the highlights are worth a brief summary. For more information, see Further Reading on p. 135.

In her Yale University study "Hands-On Science: Using Manipulatives in the Classroom" (1999), Elaine Berk found that simple manipulatives (toys such as blocks or fraction circles) kept elementary-age children involved at high levels of attention and concentration. She also found that manipulatives were beneficial to social interaction, cooperation, harmony, creativity, and self-esteem.

In 1991, educator Lydia Werbizky studied a combined grades 1 and 2 classroom. Her qualitative study found that block building enabled a variety of learning experiences, including math concepts (e.g., number, size, shape, measurement, fractions, and estimation), science concepts (e.g., balance, gravity, prediction, estimation, and experimentation), and social interaction (e.g., exchanging ideas and understanding another point of view). Block building also encouraged dramatic play, problem solving, familiarity with design and architectural forms, and self-esteem.

Studying high-school students, Patricia Ernest (1994) evaluated—in part, through students' self-reports—the effectiveness of math manipulatives (fraction circles, for example). She found that student attitudes, participation, and performance were enhanced by learning with these items.

Gina Gresham, Tina Sloan, and Beth Vinson (1997) studied the effects of instructional changes (including real-life problem solving, cooperative learning, and the use of manipulatives) on mathematics anxiety in grade 4 students. The researchers found a significant decrease in anxiety levels after the new strategies were introduced, compared to those levels before testing.

In 1985, Beth Carter used six standardized tests to measure the usefulness of directed play periods, stressing the use of puzzles, blocks, stacking toys, clay, and pounding sets. The preschool-age children who were tested were from economically depressed neighborhoods. Using California Achievement Tests, she compared these students to those who attended a traditional preschool and found that the children using the manipulatives performed better than comparable students. In addition, they scored well above grade level in reading, language, and arithmetic.

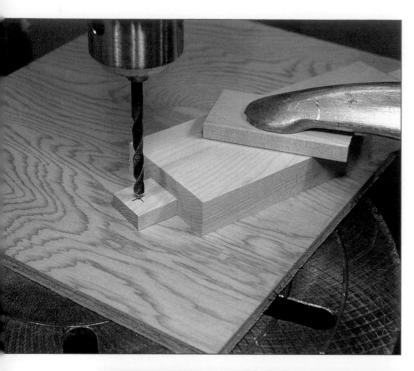

is the problem? What is the goal? What options exist? What are the pros and cons of the options? Which is the best option? Develop a few steps that are usable and appropriate.

Tips and Techniques

If you are a beginning woodworker, chances are you're a bit reluctant to run out and buy one of every tool just in case you might need it someday. Setting up shop can not only be a tricky and expensive process but also one that provides a great deal of pleasure. While each chapter includes information on necessary tools for that project, there are some general guidelines in the following section that may prove useful as you set up your shop. There are also a few general processes referred to throughout the book but discussed in more detail here. The Sources in the back of the book (see p. 130) has a section on tool and machinery suppliers, which you may find useful.

Machinery Needed

Often, as I look through books and magazines, I notice the types of shops that some craftsmen have. "Notice" is not really the correct word—perhaps "envy" is better. The shops I see are spacious and well equipped with 16-in. jointers, 24-in. planers, mortising machines, and too many fine hand tools to mention. As a machinist and a devoted woodworker, I have hopes and even plans for such a shop.

While I have a great appreciation for expensive, precision machinery, the reality is that I don't really need it, certainly not for making small projects such as the toys in this book. For light or beginning work, an inexpensive drill press and a bandsaw do much of the work. My bandsaw came with a poor blade, so I immediately purchased a better one. The drill press worked fine as it was.

If you can purchase high-quality equipment and have the room for it, by all means do so. If you cannot buy this kind of equipment for monetary or space reasons, don't let this stop you from purchasing a machine that will get the job done. Buy a smaller machine, one that the dealer will stand behind with a reasonable warranty. This approach also has the advantage of letting you use a machine for a few years as you learn which features mean the most to you and your style of woodworking.

In his excellent article "My Five Essential Power Tools" (*Fine Woodworking* 153, Winter 2001/2002), Gary Rogowski lists various considerations, including why a bandsaw is at the top of his list and a table saw is not on it at all. It is worth reading if you are about to invest in some machinery. For the projects in this book, the bandsaw should be your first purchase.

You will also need a drill press. An old machinist once told me that drilling a hole accurately is one of the most difficult operations in machining. Without a drill press, it becomes virtually impossible. Fortunately, a drill press is one of the least expensive machines, even for reasonable quality.

For these projects, a small- or medium-size disk sander—or, better yet, a disk/belt sander combination machine—will be a time-saver. It's an easy way to smooth out sawn edges. A miter gauge is an essential addition, even if it is only a simple shopmade one.

Some basic hand tools will also be needed. You may well have them on hand, but if you are about to purchase them, allow me to make a couple of suggestions. A combination set—with square head, protractor, and center head—is a versatile and valuable tool. Don't get the cheapest set around, although you don't need the precision of the best machinist's tools either. Make sure the scale, or

ruler, reads clearly and has engraved markings. A good handplane is also invaluable, and I would suggest investing in a reasonably good one (I mean a $50 plane, not a $200 heirloom).

Finally, I would suggest a couple of files. For the past 20 years, I have had the same 6-in. double-cut flat smooth file. This small file works extremely well for smoothing rough surfaces, especially on end grain. It allows you to leave a flat, accurate surface that needs minimal sanding. My second most commonly used file is a 10-in. double-cut half-round bastard file. It is great for roughing out most flat or rounded surfaces.

Gluing and Clamping

An excellent woodworker and sculptor teaching at the British Columbia Institute of Technology showed me how to glue awkward parts together by rubbing them in instead of clamping them. I was a little skeptical at first, but when I was roughing out these parts with a mallet and chisel, I found them to be extremely strong. Since then, I have not hesitated to assemble without clamping when it was impractical to clamp.

When assembling this way, use a fairly thin layer of white glue (polyvinyl acetate, or PVA) and rub

the parts with a slight side-to-side motion. With moderate pressure being applied, the glue film will grow thin and even and begin to stick. At that point, leave the glue to harden. If you have any doubt, try it out on a few scrap pieces and then break them apart. It's unlikely that they will separate along the glueline.

Where you have to close a small gap, you will need to clamp the parts. But with small toy pieces, there are many times when rubbing the part in is a better option than trying to invent some clamping method.

Finishing and Coloring

When finishing toys, safety, ease of application, and durability are the main concerns. You obviously don't want any finish that is hazardous when dry. For this reason, I have not used any stains. Urethane and varathane plastic finishes are safe when dry; most factory-made cribs have this type of finish. Some oil finishes are specifically formulated for food-contact items, and these, of course, are safe as well. Salad-bowl oil, walnut oil, and pure tung oil are approved for food-contact items.

For the toys in this book, I have used a semigloss spray urethane on parts for which I wanted to have some gloss. For most toys, however, I have used Robson's Tried & True™ Varnish Oil (linseed oil) or Original Wood Finish (linseed oil and beeswax). The linseed oil and linseed/beeswax combination are both nontoxic, with no petroleum distillates or derivatives. They are even reasonably safe to drink, although apparently large quantities may cause nausea. I haven't tried this.

The oil finishes are generally easier to apply to these toys. Oiled toys can be handled when wet, and sanding between coats is not required. Refinishing a damaged block or toy is generally more easily accomplished with an oil finish than a urethane finish.

I have also used food coloring for a few projects in this book. I like food coloring because it is safe, readily available in small quantities, and offers bright, appealing colors. The main disadvantage is that it runs and smears when it gets wet, so some form of finish needs to be applied to seal it.

When using food coloring, I've found that it works best when mixed 50/50 with water. Green can be made by mixing blue and yellow. Adjust the proportions to get the exact color you want.

Clear a large area around your project when coloring. The odd, small splash or spray can easily stray to unfinished wood, and it soaks in quickly and deeply. Where possible, I dipped the small parts into containers of coloring and then set the parts on a rack or clean paper to dry.

Fraction Circles

*m*any concepts are learned more easily with the use of manipulatives, and this is especially true of fractions. When, at an early age, a child can see and practice manipulating the various parts of a whole, the understanding that develops will be a great help when the more advanced applications are introduced farther down the road.

These eight circles use color coding to illustrate common fractions. For this set, I made the halves and the whole out of Baltic birch plywood, the thirds and sixths out of purpleheart, the quarters and eighths out of yellowheart, and the fifths and tenths out of padauk. Other woods of various colors would be just fine, or you could use the same light-colored wood for all the fractions and color them with stain or food coloring. I have also varied the thicknesses of similar-looking fractions to help differentiate them.

Many woods in 3-in. width by ¼-in. or ⅜-in. thickness are available from hobby and woodworking stores. Accordingly, I have used these measurements as the base for the Fraction Circles.

This project does not take long to make nor is it difficult. The angles of each pie-shaped piece need to be precise, but other sizing is not critical. There are 39 pieces in all; each piece is sawn to size and then sanded and finished, but the simple shapes make the process quick and easy— easy to make but a great help to anyone learning or teaching fractions.

- ☐ **Protractor, preferably from a combination set**
- ☐ **Scale (ruler)**
- ☐ **Small file (I use a 6-in. double-cut flat smooth file)**
- ☐ **Bandsaw (a small inexpensive one is adequate)**
- ☐ **Disk sander (again, a small inexpensive one will do for this project)**

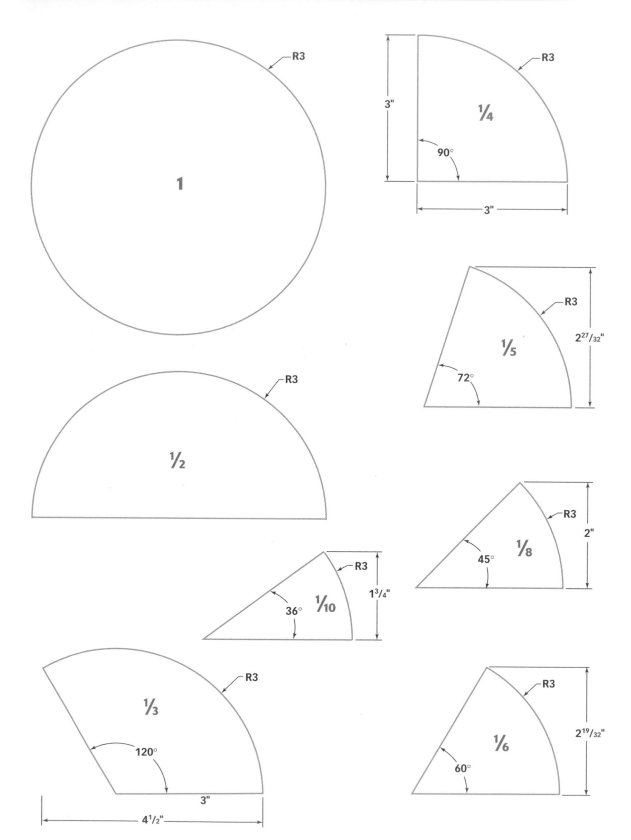

PART NAME	FINISH DIMENSIONS L X W X T	NO. REQ'D.	NOTES
Whole circle	6 in. dia. x ¼ in.	1	May use ⅜-in.-thick plywood.
Halves	6 in. x 3 in. x ¼ in.	2	May use ⅜-in.-thick plywood.
Quarters	3 in. x 3 in. x ¼ in.	4	
Eighths	3 in. x 2 in. x ¼ in.	8	
Fifths	3 in. x 2²⁷/₃₂ in. x ⅜ in.	5	
Tenths	3 in. x 1¾ in. x ⅜ in.	10	
Thirds	4 1/2 in. x 3 in. x ⅜ in.	3	
Sixths	3 in. x 2¹⁹/₃₂ in. x ⅜ in.	6	

Layout

You could draw the fractions for layout freehand, but it is easier to make templates and easier still to photocopy the templates on pp. 18 and 19. Use paper as thick as the photocopier will handle. If you must use thin paper for the templates, rub the back with pencil lead, which transforms the template into carbon paper. Make sure you space the pieces about ⅛ in. apart, enough for the saw cuts and some sanding.

1. Obtain wood the desired thickness and color. The easiest option (and probably the strongest) is to make all the pieces from Baltic birch, but I couldn't resist the visual appeal of the small strips of exotic woods. In the end, I used a bit of everything. Use whatever is convenient for you.

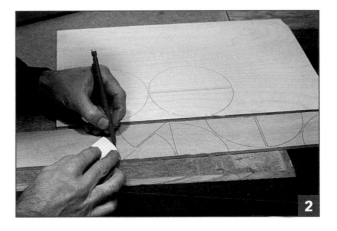

2. After you decide on a wood and a thickness for each fraction or pair of fractions (e.g., eighths and quarters), trace or lay out the outlines. While grain direction is a consideration, I haven't had any pieces break, even with grain running across the piece. Locate the parts to allow the most economical use of your wood. This will vary depending on the size of the stock you have available.

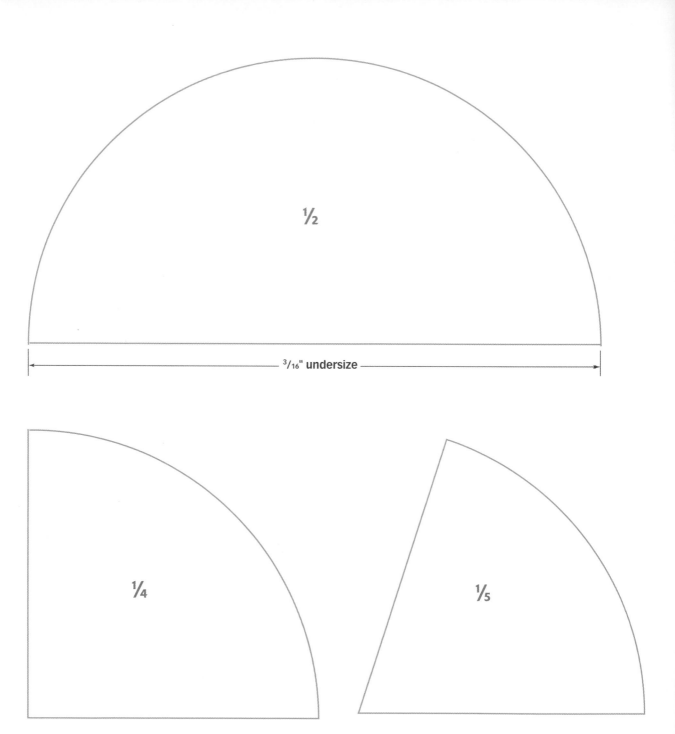

½

3/16" undersize

¼

⅕

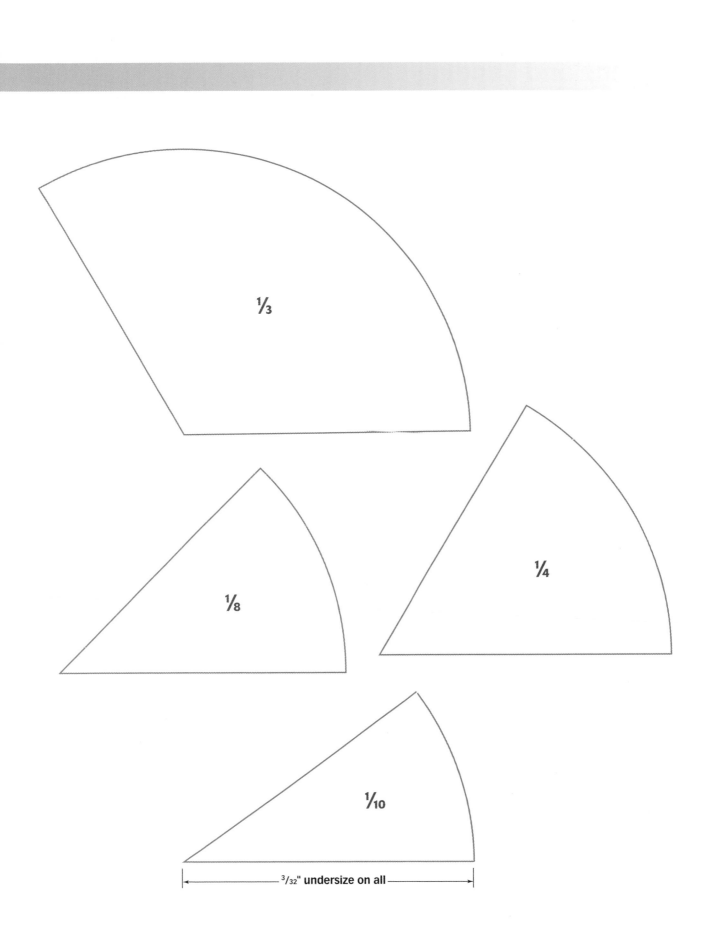

1/3

1/8

1/4

1/10

$^{3}/_{32}$" undersize on all

Cutting and Sanding

Ideally, you want to saw as close to the layout lines as possible without actually touching them. I tend to leave about ⅟₃₂ in., which gives me just enough leeway for wobbling. When sanding with a disk sander, choose a disk with fine-grit abrasive. This removes the wood a little more slowly so it is easier to keep the parts accurate, and it gives a little better finish. However, some woods burn more easily than others, so you may want to try sanding a scrap piece of each type of wood.

1. Saw out each piece, allowing enough of a margin for sanding later. I have a small, inexpensive bandsaw that I use for this operation. A scrollsaw also works well, if you have one handy. I find that a jigsaw chips the wood more than I like, but a patient person could nicely use the humble coping saw.

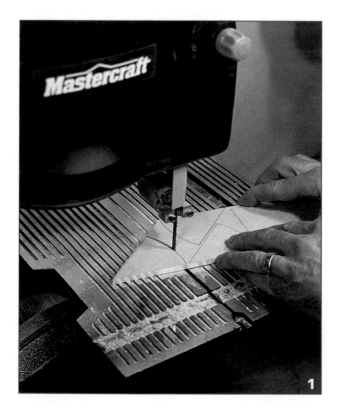

2. Use the disk sander to smooth the wood down to the line. Use a protractor to check each angle, getting as close as possible to the desired angle. If you don't have a protractor from a combination set, work to the lines as closely as possible. A smooth file works well here if you don't have a disk sander handy or find it takes off a little more wood than you like. It is best to bevel the edges slightly before filing to remove the saw marks. This reduces the tendency of the edges to splinter as you file. After filing, finish by hand-sanding (though a good smooth file will leave a surprisingly refined result).

3. Sand the corners to round them slightly. Hand-sand all surfaces to remove machining marks.

Finishing

The simplest finish for these small parts is a couple of coats of an oil finish. I tend to use tung oil, but other finishing oils work well, too. I have used a spray urethane, but it takes quite a bit of time and work to finish all the surfaces sanding between coats. Also, the smooth plastic finish tends to make small parts slippery and a little hard to manipulate.

Learning through *Play*

THESE CIRCLES are an excellent way of introducing fractions. They allow children to understand more easily how to add, subtract, and compare fractions. The different-size fraction pieces provide opportunities for ordering fractions, exploring equality and inequality of fractions, and studying common denominators. Decimals can be introduced using the tenth-size fraction pieces.

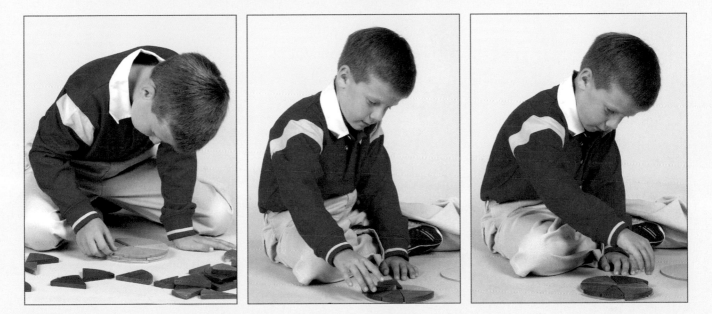

These Fraction Circles are generally used with children between grades 1 and 7, but I have even used this type of "pie" with students in grades 11 and 12 who were having difficulty working with fractions.

Young (preschool-age) kids can start by playing with these circles as puzzles, assembling each circle by choosing the pieces that fit together to make a circle. If you have them count the number of pieces required to make a complete circle, then you can explain the general concept of fractions (e.g., when there are three pieces that make up a whole, we call them "thirds," etc.).

With school-age children, you may want to start with the larger pieces—the whole circle, halves, and quarters. Show how two halves or four quarters make a whole circle and two quarters make a half circle. Demonstrate the concept of numerator and denominator. Have a youngster use quarters and halves to make ¾ or 1½,

using different methods. This would also be a good time to have kids learn how to write these fractions. Follow the same types of ideas with the smaller pieces. Illustrate the fraction ½ using as many different methods as possible (e.g., ¼, ⅙, etc.). Compare the different fraction pieces, having children organize them from smallest to largest, and identify them as tenths or fifths as appropriate.

With older children, use tenths, fifths, and halves to teach conversion to decimals. You can nicely show how a half is the same as five-tenths and a fifth is the same as two-tenths. As the kids get older, you may want to bring in other fractional or decimal systems and show how they are similar to the Fraction Circles. Money— with its quarters, dimes, and pennies—is great for this, but so is a ruler with its measurement gradations.

Pattern Blocks

kids love these geometric blocks as creative play toys. They use them to make all sorts of wonderful abstract designs, as well as recognizable faces, animals, and objects. These blocks form a sort of open-ended jigsaw puzzle, where imagination and creativity determine the outcome.

However, that's not what I had in mind when I made the first set. I thought they were a great way to learn about patterning and geometry. That is still true, but children have a lot more fun than I thought and use the blocks in many more ways than I had expected. (Note that these are small parts and not suitable for very young children, as they may pose a choking hazard.)

Pattern Blocks are simple to make, but depending on how many you want, it can take a bit of time. This is a fairly large set, and you could start with fewer pieces. The set as described here will likely take the better part of a day to make, plus finishing time.

Tools You Need

- ☐ Protractor, preferably from a combination set
- ☐ Scale (ruler)
- ☐ Small file (I use a 6-in. double-cut flat smooth file)
- ☐ Bandsaw (a small inexpensive one is adequate)
- ☐ Disk sander (again, a small inexpensive one will do for this project)

Layout

Choose a different-colored wood for each block. It is important to have contrast here, as it makes children's creations much more visually appealing and fun. As with the Fraction Circles in the previous chapter, you could use a light-colored wood for all the blocks, then color them with water colors or stain. You may want to take a look at the notes on coloring on p. 13.

The layout process is a little different for each shape. I will cover the layout of each block separately but group all the blocks to discuss instructions on sawing and sanding.

Hexagon Layout

1. Obtain wood of the desired color. I used yellowheart.

2. Draw a line parallel to a finished edge and 1¾ in. in from that edge. You will need about a 12-in. length to make five hexagons. Draw another line parallel to this one down the center (⅞ in. in from the finished edge).

PATTERN BLOCKS LAYOUT

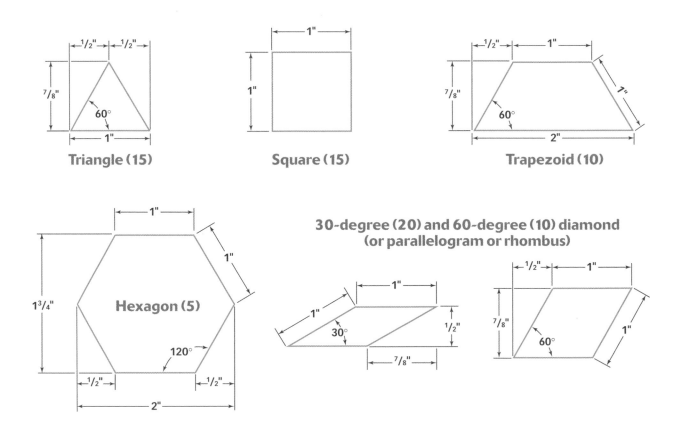

Triangle (15)

Square (15)

Trapezoid (10)

Hexagon (5)

30-degree (20) and 60-degree (10) diamond (or parallelogram or rhombus)

PATTERN BLOCKS CUT LIST

PART NAME	FINISH DIMENSIONS L X W X T	NO. REQ'D.
Triangles	1 in. x ⅞ in. x ⅜ in.	15
Squares	1 in. x 1 in. x ⅜ in.	15
Trapezoids	2 in. x ⅞ in. x ⅜ in.	10
Hexagons	2 in. x 1¾ in. x ⅜ in.	5
30-degree diamonds	1⅞ in. x ½ in. x ⅜ in.	20
60-degree diamonds	1½ in. x ⅞ in. x ⅜ in.	10

3a. Draw two sides of the hexagon, each at 60 degrees to the finished edge, which itself will form a third segment of the hexagon. Start by drawing one angled line, then measure over 1 in. along the finished edge, and draw the second angled line. Use a protractor as shown in the photo at top right.

b. You could also lay out using distances instead of angle measurements. Lay out as described in step 2, then draw a line 2 in. from the end and square to the finished edge. This will give you a rectangle 2 in. long by 1¾ in. high. Along the 2-in.-long sides, measure ½ in. in from the ends. These marks will be 1 in. apart, centered on the rectangle. These points will become the intersections for the hexagon's sides (see the photo at bottom right).

3a

3b

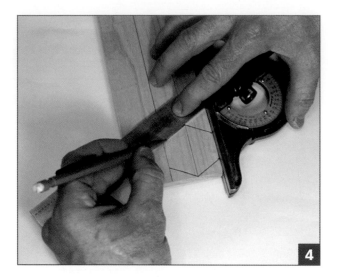

4. Draw the top half of the hexagon. To do this, draw the two 60-degree angled lines to form the top half of the hexagon, starting where the bottom angle lines intersect with the centerline.

5. Draw four more hexagons, using either the protractor or distance method. Leave enough room between pieces for a saw cut plus about ¹⁄₃₂ in. on each side for sanding and finishing.

Triangle Layout

1. Obtain wood of the desired color. I used bloodwood.

2. Square one end of the wood, and finish one edge by planing or jointing.

3. Draw a line parallel to a finished edge and ⅞ in. in from that edge. You will need about a 12-in. length to make 15 triangles.

4. On this line, measure in ½ in. from the squared end of the wood and make a small mark. On the finished edge, measure 1 in. in from the same end of the wood and make another small mark. Join these points with lines to form a triangle or use a protractor set to 60 degrees. The protractor is a little faster when doing 15 pieces, but either way is fine.

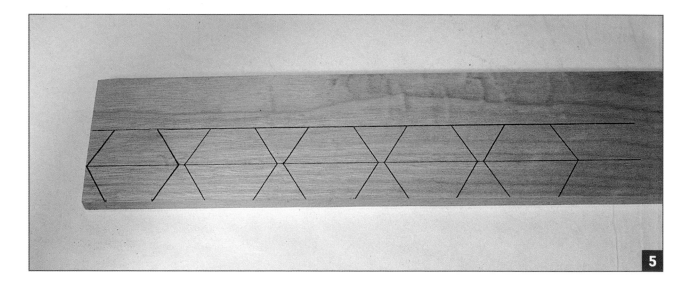

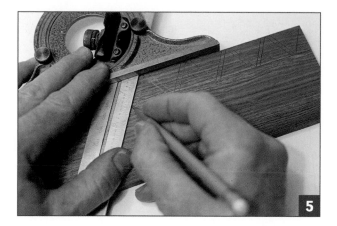

5. Leave a ⅛-in. space, and draw another line parallel to the last angled line. This leaves a little space for a cut, and starts the next (inverted) triangle.

6. Draw a 60-degree line to form the second side of this inverted triangle. If you are not using a protractor, measure over 1 in. along the line that is ⅞ in. from the finished edge, then draw the line. Each side of the triangle is 1 in. long.

7. Keep drawing triangles, alternating right side up and inverted.

Trapezoid Layout

1. Obtain wood of the desired color. I used padauk. It has a wonderful dark orange color, but its oils tend to make finishes dry slowly. Don't panic if your finish takes two or three times longer to harden than it would with other types of wood.

2. The layout for the trapezoid blocks is similar to the layout for the triangles. Draw a line parallel to a finished edge and ⅞ in. in from that edge (I'll call this line "A"). For 10 trapezoids, you'll need about an 18-in. length.

As with the triangles, using a protractor is faster, but laying out by distance measurements is also simple. Follow the drawing on p. 24 and refer to steps 3 and 4 below.

3. Using a protractor (set to 60 degrees) placed against the finished edge of the wood, draw a line to make one end of the trapezoid. Measure over exactly 2 in. along line "A" (drawn in the previous step). Draw a second line from this point angling back (as shown in the photo below) using your protractor (still set to 60 degrees), but flip the protractor over so the line is now 120 degrees to the edge of the wood.

4. Repeat the second line but leave ⅛ in. for the saw cut—this will be one side of the next (inverted) trapezoid. Measure over 2 in. along the finished edge of the wood, and draw the other side by marking a line angled 120 degrees from the edge of the wood (see photo top p. 28).

If you would like to lay out using distance measurements instead of angles, complete step 2 above. As with the triangles, the angled lines on the ends are angled over exactly ½ in. from top to bottom. The long side of the trapezoid is 2 in. long, and the short side is 1 in. long (see the drawing on p. 24).

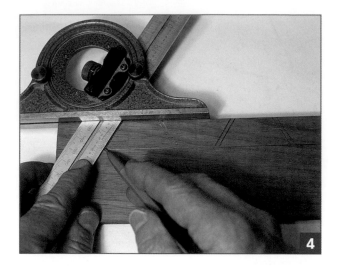

30-Degree and 60-Degree Parallelogram Layout

The layout for these two shapes is similar, so I will describe them together. There will be 20 of the 30-degree parallelograms and 10 of the 60-degree parallelograms.

1. Obtain wood of different types for these parts. I used black walnut for the 30-degree parallelogram and purpleheart for the 60-degree parallelogram.

2. For the 60-degree parallelogram, draw a line parallel to a finished edge and ⅞ in. in from that edge. You will need about a 13-in. length to make 10 pieces. For the 30-degree parallelogram, draw this line only ½ in. in from the edge; you will need about a 26-in. length (or two 13-in. pieces of wood).

3. Set the protractor to the correct angle (30 degrees or 60 degrees), and draw two lines exactly 1 in. apart.

Starting at the end of your wood, mark out the 2-in.-long distance on line "A." On the finished edge of the wood, step over ½ in. from the end, then mark out the 1-in.-long side. Joining these points will give you the angled ends of the trapezoid.

5. Keep drawing trapezoids, alternating right side up and inverted.

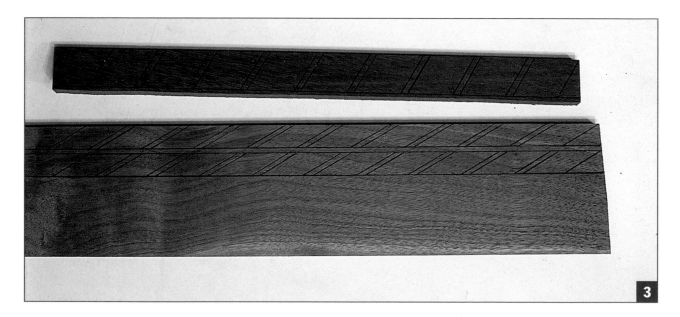

4. Leave enough space for the saw cut (about ⅛ in. for the 60-degree parallelograms and, because of the sharper angles, about ³⁄₁₆ in. for the 30-degree parallelograms), and draw another parallelogram. Continue until you have 10 of the 60-degree parallelograms and 20 of the 30-degree parallelograms.

As with the other blocks, you can lay these out using distance measurements if you desire. Follow the drawing on p. 24, and start by drawing the lines as described in step 2. The second block is set beside the first, leaving ⅛ in. between the blocks to allow for the saw cuts. For the 60-degree parallelogram, this offset is only ½ in., exactly as it is for the triangle and trapezoid. For the 30-degree parallelogram, the procedure for laying out the first block is the same, but the angled end lines are offset ⅞ in. from top to bottom to produce the sharper angle.

Square Layout

I suppose this doesn't really need any instructions. Just draw 1-in. squares, leaving about ⅛ in. between them for cutting.

Cutting and Sanding

When sawing these parts, cut as close to the line as possible without actually touching it. I leave about ¹⁄₃₂ in., which gives me a small amount of leeway for variations in the cut.

Hand-filing and -sanding is an option, but it takes quite a while with all these small parts, so I use my small disk sander. When sanding with a disk sander, choose a disk with fine-grit abrasive. This removes the wood a little more slowly so it is easier to keep the parts accurate, and it gives a little better finish. However, some woods (such as purpleheart) burn more easily than others, so you may want to try sanding a scrap piece of each type of wood first.

1. Saw out each piece, allowing a small margin for sanding.

I use my small bandsaw for this operation. A scrollsaw works fairly well, if you have one handy. A circular saw, such as table saw or miter saw, is not a good tool for this project. It is difficult to work safely with such small parts.

Learning through *Play*

PATTERN BLOCKS are intended for children from preschool to about grade 8. The smaller pieces may present a choking hazard, so very young children should not use them.

These blocks make use of children's natural creativity to introduce geometry and more complex patterning. While children are inventing shapes and patterns using these blocks, they will begin to see how common geometric shapes and angles fit together. Pattern Blocks naturally fit together in a variety of ways, and children will learn to create and understand increasingly complex patterns.

All of the following types of play will help give children a foundation for math and geometry, and will help to illustrate geometric and mathematical concepts later. To start with, describe the different geometric shapes to your children and explain how and why they fit together in different ways. You could mention things like complementary angles (two angles that add up to 90 degrees) and supplementary angles (those that add up to 180 degrees). Have children make a parallelogram using two triangles, or use different methods to produce a hexagon using triangles, parallelograms, and trapezoids.

Children could create an object that you suggest (such as a dinosaur), or they could make any object using only certain blocks (using only 15 blocks, or only triangles and squares, for example). After chil-

2. Use the disk sander to smooth the wood down to the line. Check the angles with a protractor; if you don't have one, just work to the lines as accurately as possible.

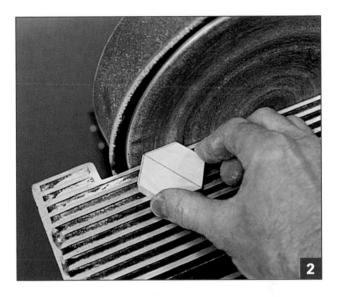

dren create a design, ask them if they can make the same shape using different blocks, tell a story about what they made, or guess the number of blocks they used.

The blocks can also be used to build walls by putting them on edge, which improves eye-hand coordination and fine-motor skills. Open-ended creative play and patterning can also be encouraged through this use.

To use Pattern Blocks to teach addition, subtraction, multiplication, and division, assign a value to each block. The basic unit is a triangle, with a value of 1. Assign, or have children determine, the value of other blocks, based on how many triangles make up each block. In this way a hexagon has a value of 6 (six triangles make up a hexagon), a large parallelogram has a value of 2, a trapezoid a value of 3, etc.

Have children make different combinations of blocks and calculate their value. For example, three parallelograms make up a hexagon, which has a value of 6. Each parallelogram has a value of 2, so 3 x 2 = 6. Any number of creations can be made, and their value calculated using basic math. Take a block away and calculate the new value. Have children create a design that has a certain value (such as 24) or an approximate value (30 to 40).

As children get older, have them calculate the value of the small parallelogram or the square, and use these in designs and calculations.

3. Sand the corners to round them slightly. Hand-sand all surfaces to remove machining marks.

Finishing

As with the Fraction Circles, the simplest finish for these small parts is a couple of coats of an oil finish. I tend to use tung oil, but other finishing oils work well, too.

■ ■ ■ ■

Big Beads

kids like stringing beads, and for such
a simple play activity, it contains a lot of learning potential.
Patterning (a premath skill) is practiced as these geometric
beads are assembled on a string in creative patterns based
on color or shape. Counting skills, color recognition, and geometric-shape
recognition can also be learned.

Making these beads is a straightforward process. The beads start out as
strips of wood, each strip a different geometric shape. These strips are then
cut up into beads and drilled. I'll explain how to make the shaped strips
for each specific bead and then cover the general processes of cutting and
drilling, which are the same for all beads.

In the next chapter (see p. 40), you'll find a project for a Bead Board.
The board consists of a simple organizer and rack that incorporates a
shape- and color-matching game as the beads are put away. If you plan to
do that project as well, make about 3 in. of extra bead material for each
shape. I'll comment on what to do with it as we go along.

Construction lumber (1½-in.-thick pine) works just fine for this process
if you do not want to purchase the more expensive maple (or other hardwood). You may also want to laminate two pieces of ¾-in.-thick wood if
you don't have a 1½-in. thickness in the type of wood you want. The
beads are designed on the basic unit of 1½ in., which allows them to be
used as blocks with the Ultimate Building Block Set (see p. 72), as well as

Tools You Need

- ☐ Small file (I use a 6-in. double-cut flat smooth file)
- ☐ Handplane, or jointer if you have one
- ☐ Awl
- ☐ Bench vise
- ☐ Bandsaw (a small one will do) or table saw
- ☐ Disk sander will be convenient (again, a small one will do)
- ☐ Drill press
- ☐ ⁵⁄₁₆-in. drill bit

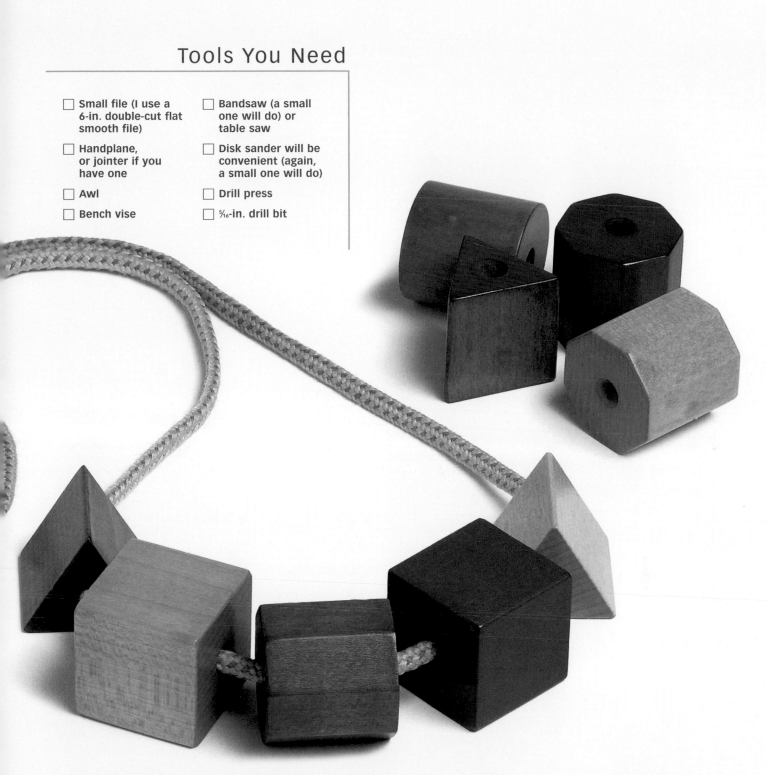

making them easy for young children to manipulate. The beads will be colored during the finishing process.

This is a great starter project—easy to do with minimal tools. Slight errors do not affect the function of the beads. You will find this a quick and enjoyable project that is low on the frustration level.

PART NAME	FINISH DIMENSIONS L X W X T	NO. REQ'D.
Triangular beads	1½ in. x 1½ in. x 1⁵⁄₁₆ in.	5
Octagonal beads	1½ in. x 1½ in. x 1½ in.	5
Square beads	1½ in. x 1½ in. x 1½ in.	5
Round beads	1½ in. dia. x 1½ in.	5

Square Bead Material

The octagonal beads will be made from square stock also, so make enough square bead material to produce the square beads and the octagonal beads (a total of 20 in., or 26 in. if you are planning to make the Bead Board in the next chapter).

1. Cut one 1⁹⁄₁₆-in.-wide strip from a 1½-in.-thick board. The finish size is 1½ in., so you are allowing about ⅟₁₆ in. for planing and smoothing.

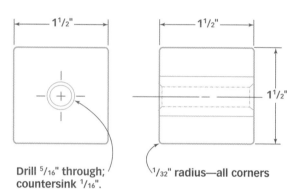

2. Plane the sawn edge smooth and to size. Check for square before you are down to the finish size, but keep in mind that being slightly out of square will not dramatically affect the toy.

Drill ⁵⁄₁₆" through; countersink ⅟₁₆".

1⁄₃₂" radius—all corners

3. If you need more strips, plane the sawn edge of the board to get a true surface, then cut another 1⁹⁄₁₆-in. strip.

4. Sand the strip that is to be used for square beads, rounding the corners slightly. Set the other length aside for the octagonal beads.

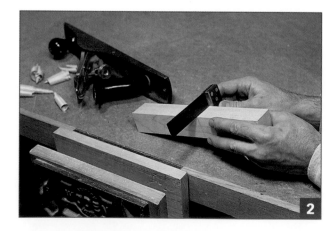

Octagonal Bead Material

Use the leftover square material that you produced in the previous section.

1. Mark out an octagon on the end of the 1½-in. square stock. Each flat will be ⅝ in. long, so measure a ⅝-in. flat centered on each side (measure in ⁷⁄₁₆ in. from each edge). Join the marks to create 45-degree bevels on the corners.

2. Put the wood in a vise, having it grip the wood on the corners, and plane the new surfaces. Measure the width of each new flat to ensure that it remains parallel.

3. Do this for each of the four new flats, ending up with an octagonal cross section.

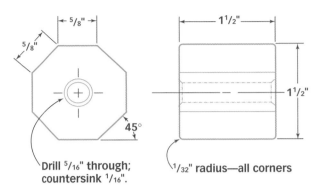

Drill ⁵⁄₁₆" through; countersink ¹⁄₁₆".

¹⁄₃₂" radius—all corners

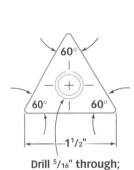
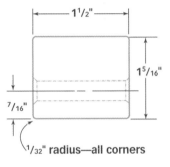

Drill ⁵⁄₁₆" through; countersink ¹⁄₁₆".

¹⁄₃₂" radius—all corners

Triangular Bead Material

Making the triangular bead stock is the most difficult of the bead material, primarily because this stock is awkward to hold in a vise for planing and finishing the edges. For this reason, I do as much finishing as possible before sawing the wood to the final triangular shape.

1. Saw a 1⅜-in.-wide strip from 1½-in.-thick wood (finish width will be 1⁵⁄₁₆ in.). You will need a 10-in.-long strip of wood (13 in. if you are making the Bead Board).

2. Plane to 1⁵⁄₁₆-in. finish width.

3. Lay out the triangular shape. Mark off a center-line on one of the ends of the strip of wood and then join a line from each of the bottom corners to the top of this centerline.

4. Saw one side of the triangle. Tilt the bandsaw table 30 degrees to suit the layout. Use a spacer (a dowel in the photo below) between the fence and the strip. Without it, the blade would hit the fence at the bottom.

5. Plane this surface flat to the line before sawing the second angle (it is much easier to hold in the vise now than it will be when both sides are sawn to 30 degrees).

6. Saw the second 30-degree angle. Cut this one as close to the line as possible because you will no longer be able to hold the part in the vise to plane it; sanding will have to do.

7. Sand each surface, rounding the corners smoothly.

ROUND BEAD LAYOUT

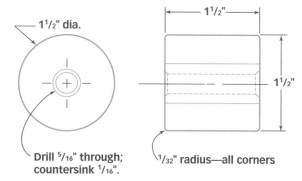

1½" dia.

Drill ⁵⁄₁₆" through; countersink ¹⁄₁₆".

1½"

1½"

¹⁄₃₂" radius—all corners

Round Bead Material

Making the round bead stock couldn't be easier. Just use 1½-in.-dia. dowel. (These beads are actually cylindrical, but the cross section is round.)

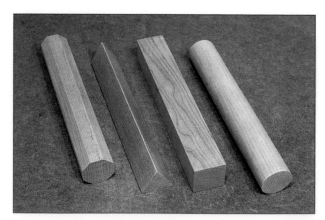

Cutting and Drilling

You could saw the beads to length using a table saw or miter saw, but I tend to use the bandsaw. It is safer with the short ends, and there's less risk of splintering on the edges. Whatever saw you use, check that the blade is exactly square to the table and that the miter gauge is also set exactly square. When drilling, keep the holes as accurate as possible. This does not affect the use at all, but it will make a difference if you make the Bead Board later.

1. Mark the beads out to length (1½ in.). If you are planning to make the Bead Board, cut the slices first (⅜ in. thick), because thin pieces are easier to cut when the material is long enough to handle safely.

2. Saw the beads about ½ in. too long. This will allow a little room for sanding on each end. Do the best you can to cut them square, because this will save filing or sanding time later.

3. If you are using a disk sander, sand the ends. Be careful not to burn them. Sand the part a little, then rotate it 60 degrees or 90 degrees, and sand it a little more. If your machine is set up with the table exactly square to the disk, this rotation will help keep the bead ends square.

Round or bevel all corners slightly (½₂ in. to ¹⁄₁₆ in.). If you don't have a disk sander, a piece of sanding belt glued to a flat surface—plywood or medium-density fiberboard (MDF)—makes a good alternative. If you don't use a sanding board or block of some type, the ends of the beads will inevitably be slightly rounded, making it frustrating to stack them (as kids are bound to do at times). If sanding by hand, don't worry too much about the exact finished length. I have also had good luck filing the end grain with a 6-in. double-cut smooth file. This small smooth file leaves a surprisingly good surface, and this approach is faster than sanding.

4. Mark the center of each bead. For the square beads, just cross the corners. This will also work with the octagonal beads. For the triangular beads, draw light lines from the center of one side to the corner opposite that side, and repeat for each corner. The three lines will intersect at the center. If you have a center head for the combination set, use it to find the center of the round beads. If not, measure across the diameter and mark a line on center, then do it again at about 90 degrees to the previous diameter location. Put a dimple in the center with an awl (or just tap a nail with a hammer). You only need to mark one end of each bead.

5. Clamp the bead in a drill press, and drill the 5/16-in.-dia. hole. Be sure the bead is sitting square on the table, with the drill-table hole or slot under the center so you can drill right through.

6. Drill through. If it is a tiny bit off center, don't worry about it.

7. Put a little bevel on each end of the hole. I do this using a portable power drill and a drill bit ground to a sharp point, but a countersink bit would be even better. Just touch the drill to the end of the hole, and use a slow speed. If you are grinding the bit yourself, it may grab a little unless you are an expert drill sharpener, so be cautious.

8. File or sand a small bevel or round on all the sharp edges and corners of each bead.

Finishing

To color the beads, I use food coloring because it is nontoxic and relatively inexpensive. See p. 13 for more information on coloring. If you are also planning to make the Bead Board, you may want to color the bead slices at the same time that you color the beads.

For this project, I used a lead-free varathane spray finish on my beads, but a salad-bowl finish is a good option as well. You need a waterproof finish to seal the coloring because food coloring is water soluble; when the beads get wet, they get messy without it. Whatever finish you use, make sure it is nontoxic when dry.

For the string, just about anything will work, but one of the nicest choices is a brightly colored shoelace. The thick lace that I used here works well because it has big, wrapped ends, making it easier to thread the beads.

Learning through *Play*

THESE BEADS present lots of opportunity for young children to improve their fine-motor skills and eye-hand coordination. They can learn patterning skills and geometric-shape identification. The beads provide occasions for counting practice and color recognition as well as to encourage creativity. They are designed for children around the age of two but could be used through age eight, depending on the child.

Have children make bead strings on their own, then let them describe to you how and why they chose certain beads. This will help them learn communication skills as well as exercise their natural creativity. It is a good idea to respond with specific, nonjudgmental comments, such as "I see you used all the red beads first, then the green ones." If you say, "It's great that you used the red ones first," then children may always do the red ones first.

Describe the geometric shapes, and have the children name the shapes as they use them. Ask them to make patterns such as: triangle, square, round, triangle, square, round, etc.; or one triangle, two squares, one triangle, two squares, etc. Colors can also be used in patterning, such as: one red, one blue, two red, two blue, etc.

Using the beads as blocks works well. Stacking the blocks into towers is great for practicing fine-motor skills. Similarly, patterns based on color or shape can also be done by stacking, especially if threading the beads is still too advanced for a young child. Have kids stack the beads by color (e.g., a pile of red beads, then a pile of yellow), by shape, or even by a combination of color and shape when the children are ready for a bigger challenge.

Lastly, let kids do whatever they want with the beads—within reason (unless you are a true anarchist). Children's free play often provides teachable moments, as well as showing adults amazingly creative ways to use toys.

Bead Board

*t*he Bead Board not only provides a neat way
to keep the Big Beads from the previous chapter in
good shape, it has excellent educational value as well.
Children learn to recognize and match the geometric
shapes of the beads to the same geometric shapes on the
Bead Board. Since both the beads and the board are colored, matching colors becomes part of the learning experience as well.

Each bead has a specific storage spot, based on color
and shape, and is located in place with a short dowel. If
you didn't already make extra bead material when you
ere making the Big Beads in the previous chapter, refer to
those instructions to create the thin slices that will provide
the pattern for putting beads on the board.

This is a quick and easy project, especially if done in conjunction
with the beads—an additional hour or two is all you'll need to complete the board. The location of the holes is fairly critical as there is only
1/16 in. between beads. If this strikes you as a bit too tight for your comfort,
allow 1/8 in. between beads.

Tools You Need

- ☐ Small file (I use a 6-in. double-cut flat smooth file)
- ☐ Awl
- ☐ Bandsaw (a small one will do) or table saw
- ☐ Drill press
- ☐ ⅜-in. drill bit

BEAD BOARD CUT LIST

PART NAME	FINISH DIMENSIONS L X W X T	NO. REQ'D.	NOTES
Triangular bead slices	⅜ in. x 1½ in. x 1$\frac{5}{16}$ in.	5	
Octagonal bead slices	⅜ in. x 1½ in. x 1½ in.	5	
Square bead slices	⅜ in. x 1½ in. x 1½ in.	5	
Round bead slices	1½ in. dia. x ⅜ in.	5	
Dowel pins	$\frac{5}{16}$ in. dia. x 1¼ in.	20	Sand dowel before cutting.
Board	10 in. x 6¼ in. x ½ in.	1	Baltic birch plywood or solid wood

Cutting and Drilling the Bead Slices

These bead slices are a little tricky to work with because they are fairly thin and fragile. Make a few extra in case one or two break, and be careful when clamping them for drilling or sanding.

1. Gather the extra bead material made in the previous chapter. If you didn't make it then, refer to the instructions (beginning on p. 34) and make 3 in. or 4 in. of each shape. Longer is better, as it allows for a better grip while sawing.

2. Mark the material to length. A ⅜-in. length works well, but there is no hard and fast reason why ¼-in. or ½-in. slices would not work, too. If the slices are any thinner, however, it makes the pieces harder to grip for sanding.

3. Saw the slices about $\frac{1}{32}$ in. too long. This will allow a little for sanding on each end. A bandsaw is the best and safest tool for this operation. Use a miter gauge to keep the wood square, as you did with the beads in the previous chapter.

4. Sand the ends. Be careful not to burn them if you are using a disk sander. Round or bevel the corners slightly on one side to break the sharp corner. The other side will be glued to the board, so a bevel is not wanted there.

5. Mark the center of each bead slice, exactly as you did with the beads (see p. 37). With an awl, put a small dimple in the center of each slice. You only need to mark one end of each bead.

6. Clamp the bead in a drill press, and drill the hole to fit a $\frac{5}{16}$-in.-dia. dowel. Be sure to clamp the slice as gently as possible and still have it hold. It is best to use the same drill size for both the bead slices and the beads.

7. Drill through.

7

Coloring the Slices

It's best to color the bead slices when you color the beads. If you have not already done so, however, refer to the coloring instructions in the previous chapter (see p. 38), using the same colors as you did for the beads.

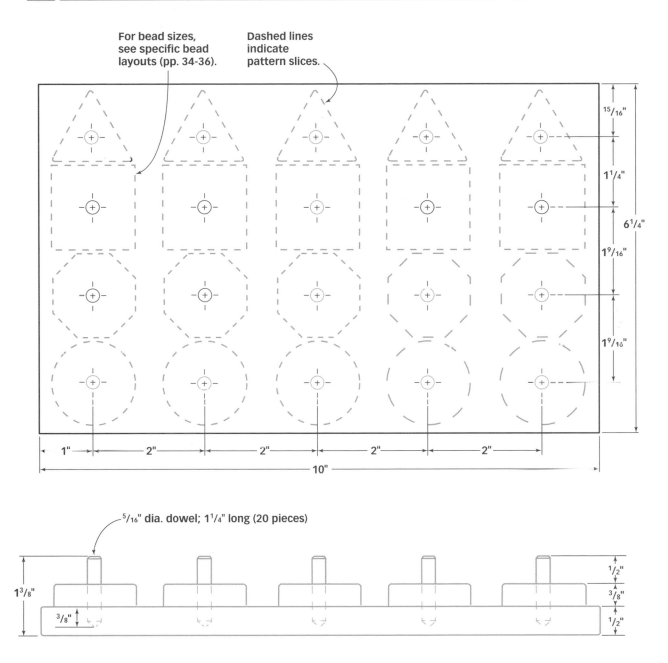

For bead sizes, see specific bead layouts (pp. 34-36).

Dashed lines indicate pattern slices.

$^{15}/_{16}$"

$1^1/_4$"

$6^1/_4$"

$1^9/_{16}$"

$1^9/_{16}$"

1"   2"   2"   2"   2"

10"

$^5/_{16}$" dia. dowel; $1^1/_4$" long (20 pieces)

$1^3/_8$"

$^3/_8$"

$^1/_2$"

$^3/_8$"

$^1/_2$"

Making the Board

1. Cut a piece of Baltic birch plywood (or other large, flat, solid wood) to 6¼ in. by 10 in. If you want to have ⅛ in. between the beads, cut the board 6⅞ in. wide instead of 6¼ in. wide.

2. Sand the edges, and bevel all the sharp corners.

3. Lay out the location of the pattern slices, referring to the drawing above. Note that the hole centers are spaced 2 in. apart along the length of the board and 1⁹⁄₁₆ in. apart along the width. There is no need to draw out the outline of each slice. Try not to draw the lines too long—just a short dash where you estimate the hole centers to be. This will save you from having to sand off the lines before finishing.

4. Mark the centers with an awl or other sharp tool.

5. Use a ⁵⁄₁₆-in. bit to drill the holes for the dowels ⅜ in. deep into the board. It is easier and looks better if you do not go right through the board. Set some form of stop so that all holes are exactly the same depth. The stop on my little press is nonexistent, so I just lower the table enough to ensure that the drill bit hits the end of its reach at the correct depth.

6. Fit the dowel to the holes in the beads and the bead slices. I had to sand the dowel material before I cut it, as it was a bit oversize.

7. Cut the dowel pieces to length, and bevel the ends slightly. On one end, this is to make them safer and, on the other end, easier to install. Make sure the dowels are the same length—it makes the board look nicer.

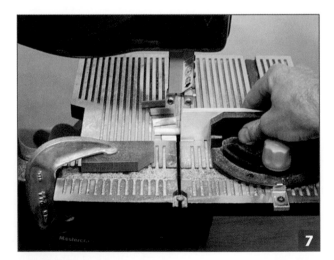

8. Glue the parts together. Use a toothpick to put glue in one hole in the board and in the hole of one bead slice. Put a little glue on the bottom face of the bead slice but not too close to the edge where it might squeeze out. Press the bead slice in place, and slide or tap the dowel into place.

Using a square, check the alignment of the bead slice. It looks best to have one edge of the square, triangular, and octagonal slices at a clean 90 degrees to the edge of the board.

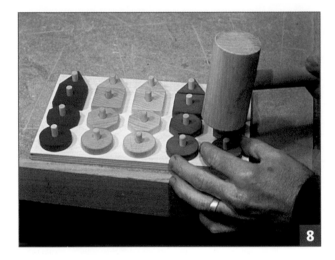

Finishing

The water-based food colors need to be sealed with a waterproof finish or the colors will eventually run and stain. It is best to apply this during the coloring process before the pieces are attached to the board.

For this board, I used a natural tung-oil finish. The board, when complete, has a lot of little nooks and corners, so it is difficult to sand between coats—something to keep in mind when choosing a finish. For this reason, I didn't use a plastic urethane finish. Whatever you decide to use, make sure it is nontoxic when dry.

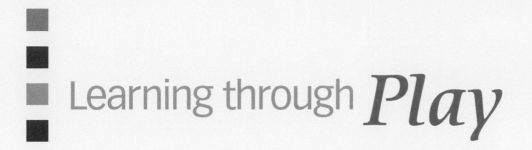

Learning through *Play*

THE BEAD BOARD, like the Big Beads, is designed for children between the ages of two and approximately eight years old, depending on the child.

Like the beads themselves, the Bead Board helps young children improve their fine-motor skills and eye-hand coordination as they fit the beads onto the short dowels. Each bead has a unique home, based on color and shape, so children learn to compare and match both the colors and the basic geometric shapes.

Talk with children about ways to compare the shapes. Count the sides, count corners, and talk about the name of each shape. Note that the round bead has no corners. Compare and match the colors as well.

If a child is having trouble matching both shape and color, you may want to concentrate on just one characteristic—either color or shape. You may even find that with young children, just having them put the beads onto the pegs is enough of a challenge. In this case, don't add the potential frustration of matching until the child is ready.

Attribute Dominoes

Years ago our family was given a box of huge dominoes, nicely made from 2x4 pine. The children used these endlessly (and still do). Mostly they were used to build large structures that were admired and then knocked down with a great crash. As we'll see in the Ultimate Building Block Set chapter, this has merit in its own right, but dominoes' traditional use has educational value as well.

This variation of dominoes is geared to teach attributes of shape and color. While played in the same way that traditional domino games are played, the players match geometric shapes, sizes, colors, or some combination of the above. This allows young children to play while ensuring that older players enjoy the game.

Since the size of these dominoes is based on the basic unit of 1½ in., they can be incorporated into the Ultimate Building Block Set. You can make the tiles out of 2x4 pine or fir or out of hardwood. The hardwood version costs more and requires more planing and sizing, but it will resist denting better than softwood. For this project, I used local birch, which was an inexpensive option for me. However, our pine set has survived many years of use and is still functional. If you want a smaller set of dominoes, reduce all the sizes by half. The resulting 1½-in.-wide by 3-in.-long dominoes may be made of ¾-in.-thick solid wood.

The attached geometric shapes are made from thin veneer, available at hobby shops and catalog companies, such as Lee Valley Tools.

Tools You Need

- ☐ Bandsaw (a small, inexpensive one is adequate) or table saw
- ☐ Sharp scissors
- ☐ Parallel or "C" clamps (two or three will do)
- ☐ Handplane, or a jointer if you have one
- ☐ Disk sander will be convenient (again, a small one will do)

I used a light-colored veneer and dyed it with food coloring to obtain different colors.

This project is not difficult to make but does take a while because there are 21 dominoes, each with two shapes attached. All told, it will probably take you a couple of days to complete this project.

PART NAME	FINISH DIMENSIONS L X W X T	NO. REQ'D.	NOTES
Tiles	6 in. x 3 in. x 1½ in.	21	Thickness includes veneer shapes.
Large veneer triangles	2³⁄₁₆ in. x 1⅞ in. x ¹⁄₃₂ in.	7	
Large veneer circles	2 in. dia. x ¹⁄₃₂ in.	7	
Large veneer squares	2 in. x 2 in. x ¹⁄₃₂ in.	7	
Small veneer triangles	1⁵⁄₆₄ in. x ¹⁵⁄₁₆ in. x ¹⁄₃₂ in.	7	
Small veneer circles	1 in. dia. x ¹⁄₃₂ in.	7	
Small veneer squares	1 in. x 1 in. x ¹⁄₃₂ in.	7	

DOMINO TILE LAYOUT

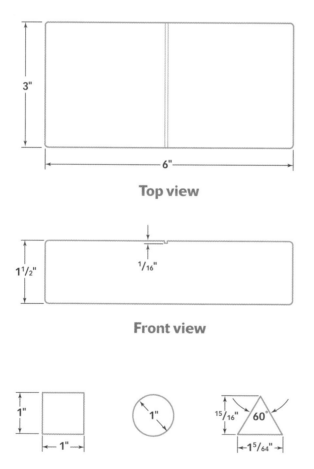

Top view

Front view

Small veneer shapes

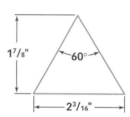

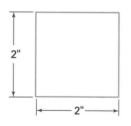

Large veneer shapes

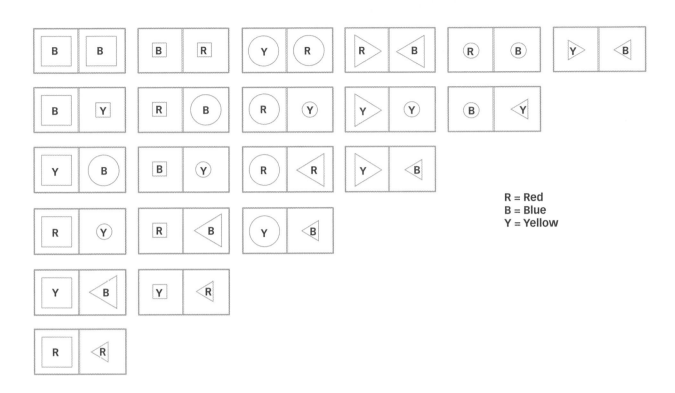

R = Red
B = Blue
Y = Yellow

Domino Tiles

These blank rectangular blocks provide the base for the dominoes; when they are made and sanded, you will glue on the veneer shapes.

Make 21 tiles and 42 veneer shapes. This number of tiles allows for every combination of pairs of size and shape. There will be six different geometric objects composed of three shapes, two sizes of each. To add the attribute of color, these shapes will be dyed red, yellow, or blue (you could use different colors, of course).

1. Cut the stock to width if using 2x4 construction lumber. Carefully saw the wood to just over 3 in. wide and then plane to 3 in. exactly.

2. Lay out the tiles to length. Do this as carefully as possible so that all the domino tiles will be the same size. Variations in size of more than ½2 in. make the tiles less useful for stacking or for use as building blocks, although they still work just fine as dominoes.

3. Cut the tiles to length, adding about ½2 in. for sanding the ends. After cutting the long boards to a reasonably short length, I use the miter gauge on my little bandsaw. It is a big cut for a small saw so

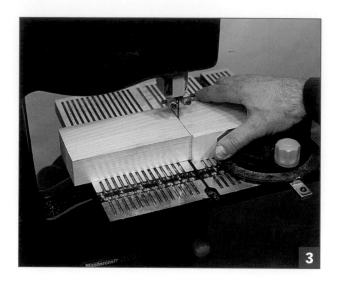

if you do it this way, feed the wood in slowly. If you have a miter saw, use it with a stop to keep all the tiles the same length.

4. Sand the edges and ends as needed. If using a disk or belt sander choose a fine-grit disk or belt, and check frequently for accurate length and squareness of the ends. You could do this sanding by hand as well, starting with a coarse grit.

5. Saw a 1/16-in.-wide by 1/16-in.-deep slot down the center of each tile. This will mark off the two halves of the domino. Do this on the best face of the tile. You could use the bandsaw as shown in the photo below, but a handsaw would also work well.

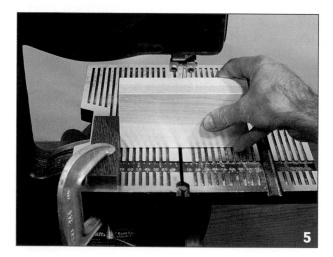

6. Sand all sharp corners, and sand the faces of the tiles as needed.

Veneer Shapes

On occasion I have sawn very thin strips, cut and glued them in place, and then sanded them flat and smooth. However, using purchased veneer is much easier and quicker than making your own. Use light-colored veneer for all the shapes and then color them with food coloring before gluing them to the tiles.

1. Lay out the veneer for the three shapes, each shape in the two sizes. Cut eight of each (you only need seven, but one extra is a good idea because these veneer parts are fragile).

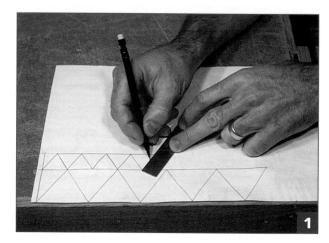

The layout for the square and round shapes is easy. Use a square and ruler for the square shape, and a compass for the round shape. Since you will be cutting with a razor knife or scissors, you don't need to leave any space between the squares, but a small gap (maybe 1/8 in.) between the circles makes the cutting a little easier.

To lay out the large triangles, draw parallel lines 1⅛ in. apart and about 10 in. long. On the bottom line, measure out four 2³⁄₁₆-in. distances. On the top line, start out half this distance in from the end, to locate the top point of the first triangle (1³⁄₃₂ in. from the end). From there, step off four 2³⁄₁₆-in. distances. Join the dots, and you should have eight triangles. Lay out the small triangles the same way but half the size (half of 1³⁄₃₂ is ³⁵⁄₆₄). On my layout, these are just above the large triangles.

2. Cut the shapes using sharp scissors. Since the veneer is brittle and fragile, you may want to wet down the area you will be cutting. After soaking for about a minute, the wood will cut much better.

3. When dry, lightly sand the edges. Watch for the fragile tips of the corners of the triangle; you may want to flatten them off slightly.

4. Dye the shapes, and let them dry. You may sand a little after coloring, as the color soaks right through most thin veneer. For this project, I used red, yellow, and blue coloring. Each color is applied to two large and two small shapes, for a total of twelve objects per color. It takes 42 pieces to have every combination of size and shape paired off on the tiles. This will leave you with six leftover pieces, which you can color as you wish. For coloring hints, see p. 13.

Assembly

1. Glue the shapes to the dominoes. Spread glue on one side of the veneer shape. Use a small brush to get the glue right up to the edges. I thin the glue slightly (1 part water to 4 parts glue) so it spreads evenly and thinly. It is a good idea to try gluing a sample of veneer to scrap wood, ensuring that the glue is adequate but not squeezing out a lot when clamped.

Clamp using a small, flat board over the shape. Use something that the glue will not stick to if it soaks through the veneer a bit. I use melamine, but covering the clamping block with plastic wrap or waxed paper will also work.

2. When the glue is hard, remove the clamps and carefully remove any excess glue using a small chisel or a razor knife.

3. Sand the veneer shapes lightly. Make sure there are no sharp corners anywhere on the domino tile.

Finishing

Finish as desired. I have sometimes used a natural tung-oil finish. It takes a while to dry and isn't glossy, but it is nontoxic wet or dry. It is easy to sand out scratches and add a little more oil if natural wear and tear makes this necessary. On this set, I decided to use a plastic finish, of the type often used on baby cribs. This urethane is nontoxic after it hardens and provides a hard finish.

I have one set of dominoes that has wax only, and that works well also but doesn't darken the wood in the way an oil or wet type of finish does. Whatever you put on, check that it is nontoxic.

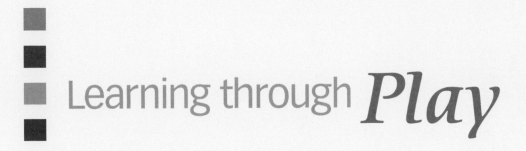

Learning through *Play*

THESE DOMINOES are intended for children ages two and up. There is no real age limit, but my children rarely used them after the age of about 12.

Attribute dominoes help children develop recognition and understanding of the attributes of shape, color, and size. Children also help develop fine- and gross-motor skills when the dominoes are used to build towers or in "knockdown" rows. And letting children play with dominoes in a free manner enhances creativity, as children invent all sorts of structures and games.

To enhance the educational value, take the time to talk about the different geometric shapes. Describe the number of sides and angles of each, and teach the names of the shapes. Even young children will easily learn the correct names when they're taught through play.

A variety of matching games can be played with attribute dominoes, just as with traditional dominoes. Matching may be done on the basis of:

- Shape only (disregarding color and size)
- Color only (disregarding shape and size)
- Size only (disregarding shape and color)
- Shape and size but color is different
- Color and size but shape is different
- Shape and color but size is different
- Shape, color, and size

There are almost endless ways to use dominoes, and it is worth reading instructions for domino games. These can be found in inexpensive domino sets, in library books, or on the Internet.

Attribute Dominoes   53

Shape Puzzle Box

i made a little box like this for my son Eric when he was a toddler. The next two children also played with it, and it has survived in fine condition. The box consists of three layers, each with a hole in the center. The holes are three different shapes: square, triangle, and circle. A hinged lid tops the box, and a thin slab forms the bottom.

Inside, three wooden shapes with small handles fit into the shaped holes. A child learns to open the lid and place the three blocks into the corresponding layer in the box. This needs to be done in the right order, so that the smallest shape, the triangle, goes in first followed by the slightly larger circle, and finally the square. The triangular and square blocks need to be rotated to fit in place. The box can then be closed. There is nothing stopping you from adding another shape (four layers), changing the shapes, or adding a latch to the lid.

This rewarding project is especially fun to make. There are only a few parts, sizes are not critical, and the fit of the puzzle pieces to the box is very loose, as it needs to be for children. Fitting hinges always takes a little care, but aside from that, the project is uncomplicated. Even if you miss a size or two, the puzzle can still work wonderfully. Making the puzzle box will likely take about half a day plus finishing time.

Tools You Need

- ☐ Scale (ruler)
- ☐ Square
- ☐ Compass
- ☐ Awl
- ☐ Coping saw
- ☐ Small file (I use a 6-in. double-cut flat smooth file)
- ☐ Medium-size file (such as an 8-in. double-cut flat bastard file)
- ☐ Handplane
- ☐ Parallel or "C" clamps, with at least a 3-in. opening (three or four will do)
- ☐ Drill press
- ☐ ¼-in. drill bit
- ☐ Sanding drum (1 in. or 2 in. dia.) for the drill press
- ☐ Disk sander will be convenient
- ☐ Bandsaw (a small inexpensive one is adequate)

Box Layers

The box consists of three layers. The layers are ¾-in.-thick square boards, with a different shaped hole cut out of each one.

1. Cut three squares, about 5⅛ in. by 5⅛ in., from a ¾-in.-thick board. The box will end up close to 5 in. square by the time the three layers are glued together and the edges are trimmed even. Don't sand any edges yet—it is best to do this after the box is assembled.

2. Lay out the square hole, but don't lay out the holes for the other two shapes until later. Reference the lines from one straight edge, using a ruler and a square to measure from this edge only. Start at the center of your 5⅛-in. by 5⅛-in. square, and lay out lines 1½ in. on each side of the centerlines.

After the square hole is cut out and sanded to its final shape and size, you will trace this onto the second layer. The size of the circle is based on the final size of the square, and the size of the triangle is based on the size of the circle. Doing it this way leaves some room for variation in case a part ends up slightly over or under the intended size.

3. Lay out ¼-in.-dia. holes at each corner. Have the center of the hole ⅛ in. from the line, so that the edge of the hole ends up exactly on the line. Mark the center of each hole with an awl.

4. Drill the holes. Have the part clamped onto a scrap of wood so that it doesn't splinter.

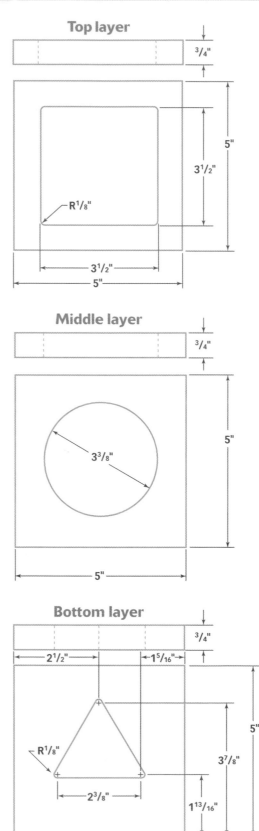

Top layer

¾"

5"

3½"

R⅛"

3½"

5"

Middle layer

¾"

5"

3⅜"

5"

Bottom layer

¾"

2½"

1⁵/₁₆"

5"

R⅛"

3⅞"

2⅜"

1¹³/₁₆"

5"

PART NAME	FINISH DIMENSIONS L X W X T	NO. REQ'D.	NOTES
Box lid	5 in. x 5 in. x ½ in.	1	Cut ⅛ in. over length and width; trim later.
Layers	5 in. x 5 in. x ¾ in.	3	Cut ⅛ in. over length and width; trim later.
Bottom	5 in. x 5 in. x ⅛ in.	1	Use Baltic birch plywood. Cut ⅛ in. over length and width; trim later.
Square puzzle piece	3¼ in. x 3¼ in. x ⅛ in.	1	Baltic birch plywood
Round puzzle piece	3⅛ in. dia. x ⅛ in.	1	Make diameter to fit—about 3⅛ in.
Triangular puzzle piece	2⁵⁄₁₆ in. x 2 in. x ⅛ in.	1	Size to fit round layer.
Handles	1 in. x ¾ in. x ½ in.	3	

5. Lay out the square on the back side as well, using the hole edges as references. This will help you saw accurately.

6. Cut along the lines using a coping saw. Be careful to have the saw cut square to the part, not at an angle. It is a good idea to cut about ¹⁄₆₄ in. to ¹⁄₃₂ in. from the line to allow for some filing and sanding.

7. File and sand these inside surfaces straight and square, except where the drill bit left a radius in the corners of the square cutout. If, by mistake, you file into these rounded corners, just carry on doing so, to get a sharper corner. If you can leave the slight radius, do that. If you are using a coarser file to start with, watch for splintering on the end grain. You may need to use lighter strokes or a finer file. The side with splinters, if any, can be put facedown so that these splinters will not be seen, but you need at least one good side.

8. Trace the finished square onto the next layer.

9. Find the center of this drawn square, and use it as the center for the circle. Set the compass to draw a circle about ¼ in. smaller in diameter than the penciled square (the compass setting should be about 1¹¹⁄₁₆ in. radius).

10. Drill a hole along the edge of the circle. Again, have the edge of the hole lined up with the edge of the layout line. You may want to draw the circle on the back as well. To do this, measure carefully to locate the center.

11. Using the coping saw again, saw around the circle, then file and sand to the line as you did with the first layer, or use a sanding drum on the drill press. I like the sanding drum option, but don't push too hard as the drill-press quill is not designed for continually high degrees of side force.

12. Trace the circle onto the last layer.

13. With a compass set to the radius of that circle, step off six times around the circumference. Start at the top of the circle so that the triangle does not end up at an odd angle to the square. If the compass is still set to the exact radius, it will step off exactly six times. Starting with the mark at the top of the circle, use every other mark as a corner of the triangle, and draw the triangle.

14. Lay out for a hole in each corner but set in ⅛ in. so that the edge of the hole will just touch the two lines that form the corner.

15. Drill the holes.

16. As with the square and circle, cut out the triangle. File and sand.

Puzzle Pieces

These are the three shapes that fit into the box. They are made of ⅛-in.-thick Baltic birch plywood, with small handles glued on.

1. Lay out the three puzzle pieces. In the end, there should be a ⅛-in. gap all around when each piece fits into the box. Trace the cutouts from the box layers, then measure in ⅛ in. all around.

PUZZLE PIECE LAYOUT

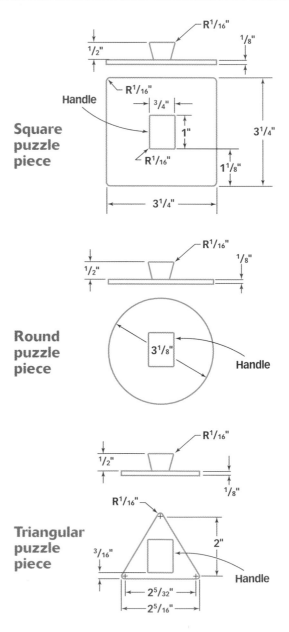

2. Cut to size, and sand the edges as needed.

3. Cut a strip of wood, ½ in. thick by ¾ in. wide, for the handles. For this project, I used a strip of purpleheart, because it was handy and provided a little color. It only needs to be about 3 in. long, but a little extra makes it easier to plane.

4. Lay out the slope on the sides. Plane to get the angle on each side so that the bottom of the strip is only about ½ in. wide while the top remains ¾ in. wide.

5. Sand as needed, rounding the sharp top edges a little.

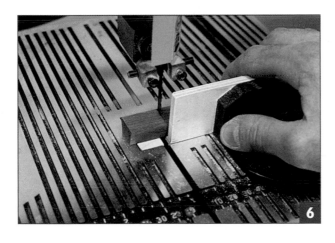

6. Lay out and cut the handles to length.

7. File and sand as needed, rounding all sharp corners and edges.

Lid and Bottom

These are just two squares of wood, each piece the same size as the middle layers. They will be trimmed and sanded to their exact size later.

Cut the parts to 5⅛ in. square, just like the box layers. Use ⅛-in.-thick plywood for the bottom and ½-in.-thick solid wood for the lid. Both of these parts could be a little thicker if that is more convenient for you. Screws will be put into the lid to attach the hinges, so the thickness may depend on which type and size of hinge you use.

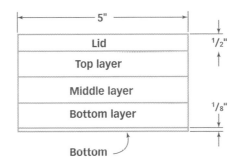

Assembly and Finishing

1. Center the handles on the puzzle pieces by measuring in from each side. Make a couple of small pencil dots (barely visible) to mark the location, keeping in mind these dots cannot be easily removed later. Centering the handle on the triangle is more of a judgment call; just locate it so it looks right. This probably means having it about 3⁄16 in. from one edge and parallel to that edge (see the drawing on facing page).

Spread a small amount of glue on the handles and clamp them gently to the puzzle pieces, checking that they don't slide out of place. You may want to

slide the handles over ¼₄ in. or so, to just cover the tiny pencil dots.

2. Sand the box layers, especially any surfaces that will be seen in the interior of the box later.

3. Assemble the three box layers and the bottom. It is best to put glue on the bottom of the layers only, keeping the glue back from the interior edges. If you put glue on the tops of the layers, it is harder to define exactly where the glue should go, and it will be difficult to remove excess glue later.

Clamp the parts together, aligning and centering the internal shapes carefully. Align the inside contours, but don't worry about lining up the outside surfaces. I put a scrap block under the bottom to even out the clamping pressure.

4. When the glue is hard, lay out a cutting line ¾ in. out from the inside edge of the cutout, on all four sides. If ¾ in. does not work well, adjust the size until it does, but keep it even on all sides.

5. Carefully saw to the line, using the bandsaw. This is a thicker cut, so if you are using a small bandsaw, feed the piece through slowly and carefully.

6. Sand all the surfaces flush and square. I use a disk/belt sander for this, but it could be done with a file and sandpaper, though this would take longer.

7. Trim the lid to the size of the box, and sand all surfaces.

8. Finish the box and the lid separately. For this project, I sprayed on three coats of urethane plastic finish, sanding lightly between coats. Do the same with the puzzle pieces.

9. Attach the hinges. For this project, I kept this as simple as possible, with the piano hinge being surface mounted. You can chisel in hinges if you desire. If you do so, do the job carefully; even a little inaccuracy here produces an unsightly result.

Learning through *Play*

THE SHAPE PUZZLE BOX is particularly suitable for toddlers because it helps develop gross- and fine-motor skills through the careful placement of the puzzle pieces. As the child advances, simple geometry is introduced as the shapes become recognizable and familiar. The latching device, if simple, also develops fine-motor skills. Through all this, problem-solving processes are developed. Counting to three or four can be learned or reinforced as the three- and four-sided shapes are described.

As you start to play with your little one, open the lid for him or her. Show one shape at a time and demonstrate how it fits. Have the child try. Talk about the shape, calling it by name (triangle, circle, and square) and describing it in simple terms. For example, show how the triangle has three corners, then count them out. Do the same with the triangular hole it fits into. Talk a little about circles, perhaps pointing out that they have no straight sides, which allows them to roll like a wheel or ball. You may even want to point out the difference between a circle and a sphere, if you have a ball to show and compare.

When the child becomes familiar with the box, show how the catch works, and how the lid hinges up.

Although the lid is small and light, illustrate how it could pinch if a finger was left near the hinge as the lid is closed. Better to learn this here than with a car or house door.

Don't forget to leave some room for divergent (open-ended) learning. What other things fit into the box? This will give you the opportunity to talk about concepts such as long and short, thick and thin, and big and small. You may end up finding other things that are round or triangular or square that will fit. See what kids come up with, and talk about why each item either fits in the box or doesn't.

Stacking Pyramid

building with blocks is a popular pastime for children of all ages, and this toy allows young children to make a pyramid tower that doesn't fall over. To provide a challenge to the toddler, however, each block must be put on in order or it won't fit on the central pillar, which is itself a pyramid shape. You can provide hints by using different-colored blocks in a pattern or by using two colors and alternating them as I have done here. The two-color approach seems to work best because young children tend to have trouble with more complicated patterns.

The toy consists of a slender pyramid-shaped pillar attached to a square base. Six blocks stack onto the pillar, each a little smaller (and with a smaller square-shaped hole) than the last. This means that the small blocks cannot slide down to the bottom of the pillar, ensuring that the blocks are stacked in order.

Choose hard, strong wood for this project. I use maple if I am coloring the wood; otherwise I use maple for the light-colored wood and black walnut or purpleheart for the darker wood.

This is a little more difficult than the projects in the previous chapters, but even sanded nicely, it can be done in a couple of days. Filing and fitting the blocks to the pillar takes a bit of careful handwork and is the most difficult and time-consuming part of the project. If you have ¾-in.-thick wood, simple machine work is all that is required.

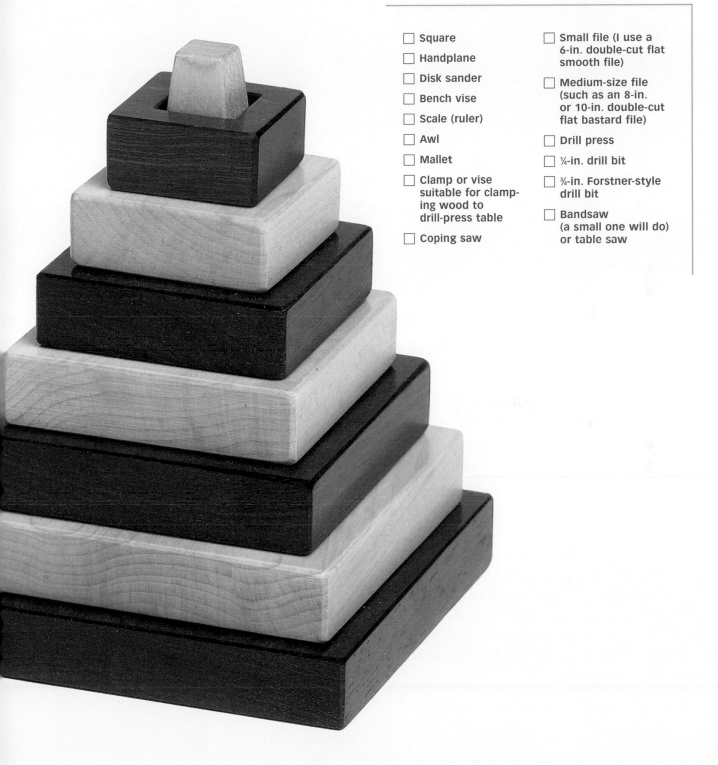

Tools You Need

- ☐ Square
- ☐ Handplane
- ☐ Disk sander
- ☐ Bench vise
- ☐ Scale (ruler)
- ☐ Awl
- ☐ Mallet
- ☐ Clamp or vise suitable for clamping wood to drill-press table
- ☐ Coping saw
- ☐ Small file (I use a 6-in. double-cut flat smooth file)
- ☐ Medium-size file (such as an 8-in. or 10-in. double-cut flat bastard file)
- ☐ Drill press
- ☐ ¼-in. drill bit
- ☐ ¾-in. Forstner-style drill bit
- ☐ Bandsaw (a small one will do) or table saw

PART NAME	FINISH DIMENSIONS L X W X T	NO. REQ'D.	NOTES
Pillar	5 in. x 1½ in. x 1½ in.	1	
Base	4½ in. x 4½ in. x ¾ in.	1	Alternate light and dark wood for base and stacking blocks.
Stacking block 1	1½ in. x 1½ in. x ¾ in.	1	
Stacking block 2	2 in. x 2 in. x ¾ in.	1	
Stacking block 3	2½ in. x 2½ in. x ¾ in.	1	
Stacking block 4	3 in. x 3 in. x ¾ in.	1	
Stacking block 5	3½ in. x 3½ in. x ¾ in.	1	
Stacking block 6	4 in. x 4 in. x ¾ in.	1	
Joint dowel	1½ in. x ¾ in. dia.	1	Cut ¹⁄₁₆ in. longer; trim after assembly.

Pillar

This pillar is the center post that locates the six blocks. It is 5½ in. long and has a square cross section, tapering from 1½ in. wide at the bottom to ½ in. wide at the top. It will be attached to the base later.

1. For the pillar, laminate two pieces of ¾-in.-thick wood, or use 1½-in.-thick wood if you have it. Cut a block 1½ in. by 1½ in. at least 5½ in. long.

2. Square up the block by planing the edges as needed. Having it square now will make it easier to keep it square as you start to taper it.

3. Saw the ends to length and square them up carefully, especially the end that will be on the bottom. I cut the ends on a bandsaw or miter saw, then touch the ends to a disk sander that has the table set exactly square to the disk. Sand a little, rotate the block 90 degrees, and sand a bit more. Do this several times as you square it up, and the result should be satisfactory. Get it as close as you can to the finish dimensions.

4. Lay out for the taper on two sides. Use the end that is the most square as the large end.

5. Cut the taper on the bandsaw. Make the first two cuts leaving ½ in. or so uncut so the layout on the other side isn't sawn off (see the photo top right). Then make the two cuts on the other side, completing the cut (see the photo bottom right). Finish off the first two cuts, by eye. Save the wedge-shaped pieces for the next step.

5a

5b

6. Plane or sand the tapered surfaces. To hold the pillar in a vise, use the two discarded wedges cut from the sides.

Check regularly for squareness. This can be tricky. It is easy to check at the large end of the pillar, but along its length, make sure you hold the square so it measures perpendicular to the centerline of the pillar (see the drawing p. 66).

Also, make sure the angled surfaces are as straight as possible. Exact size is nice, but the stacking blocks

STACKING PYRAMID LAYOUT

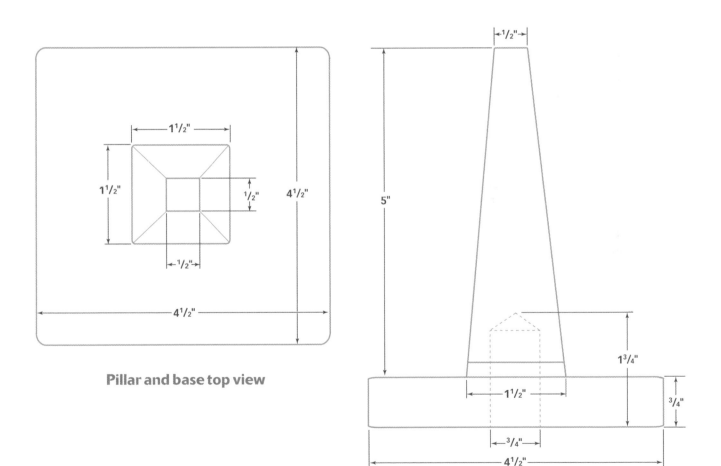

Pillar and base top view

Pillar and base front view

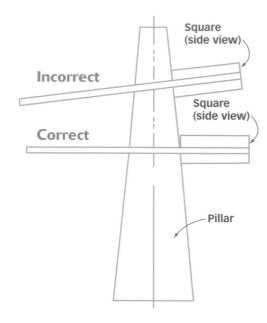

Square
(side view)

Incorrect

Square
(side view)

Correct

Pillar

will be fitted to your tapered pillar, so accuracy is not as important as squareness.

7. Round the corners slightly (⅟₁₆ in. to ⅟₃₂ in. radius) except for the end where the pillar will attach to the base.

8. Lay out for the stacking blocks on the pillar. Do this by measuring ¾-in. increments up from the bottom. Draw lines across, indicating where the different blocks should fit. You will use these lines later to file the square holes to the correct size, allowing each block to slide down at least as far as the corresponding line.

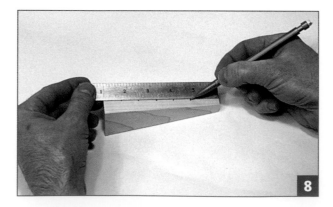

Stacking Blocks and Base

Each block is a ¾-in.-thick square, with a square hole in the center. The base is a similar block but without the hole. The blocks need to fit with either side up, so the holes are angled from the top and from the bottom. This is actually easier than designing them to fit from one side only.

1. Lay out the outside sizes for all the square blocks and for the base, all on ¾-in.-thick wood. For this project, I have alternated light and dark wood. Do not lay out the square holes yet. Reference all the layout lines from a straight, planed edge. Use a square and ruler to get all measurements from this true surface.

Front view

Top view

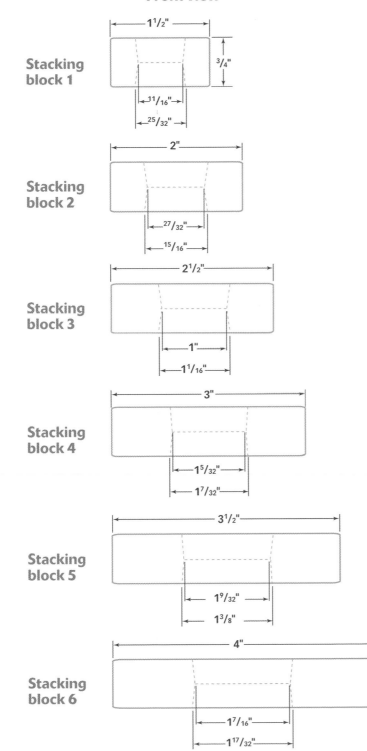

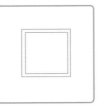

Note: All stacking blocks are ¾-in. thick and are square when viewed from the top (like the top view of the small layer above).

Stacking block 1

1¹/₂"
³/₄"
1¹/₁₆"
²⁵/₃₂"

Stacking block 2

2"
²⁷/₃₂"
¹⁵/₁₆"

Stacking block 3

2¹/₂"
1"
1¹/₁₆"

Stacking block 4

3"
1⁵/₃₂"
1⁷/₃₂"

Stacking block 5

3¹/₂"
1⁹/₃₂"
1³/₈"

Stacking block 6

4"
³/₄"
1⁷/₁₆"
1¹⁷/₃₂"

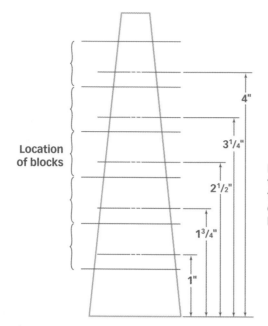

Location
of blocks

4"

3¹/₄"

Measure at
these places
to get size
of block hole
layout.

2¹/₂"

1³/₄"

1"

2. Saw the blocks to size, leaving only about ¹/₃₂ in. for sanding on the edges. I cut these using my little bandsaw, but I am pretty careful to make the cuts as straight as possible.

3. Sand the edges smooth, and square them to the original

reference edge in step 1. Bevel the edges to about ¹/₁₆ in. It is probably best to bevel them by hand unless you have a sensitive touch on the disk sander.

4. Lay out the square holes using the pillar as a guide (see the drawing above). If your pillar did not end up the same size as indicated in the drawing, you should check the hole size by measuring the width of the pillar at a point ¹/₈ in. lower than where the center of the block will be

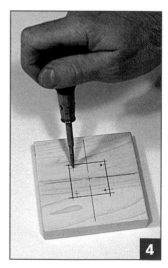

(you want the blocks to be able to slide ¹/₁₆ in. to ¹/₈ in. below the line).

To lay out the square holes, work from the center and measure out from there. This ensures that the holes will be centered on the block, regardless of block size or pillar size.

5. Lay out for a ¼-in.-dia. drilled hole in each corner. Measure ⁵⁄₃₂ in. in from each line. This will locate the edge of the hole ¹⁄₃₂ in. from the layout, leaving a little bit of room for fitting later. Mark the center of each hole with an awl or other sharp tool.

6. Drill the holes. Clamp the block onto a piece of scrap wood so that the drill bit does not splinter the wood as it breaks through. If you are using a vise for the small blocks, have the block pressed down on a scrap piece.

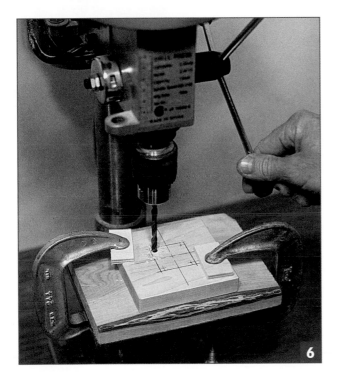

7. Using the holes as references, mark the layout lines on the back surface, exactly as they are in the front. This will help you keep the saw cut accurate and square.

8. Saw the blocks using a coping saw. Install the blade through a hole and reassemble the coping saw. Cut about ¹⁄₃₂ in. from the line. Use gentle down pressure, checking front and back to keep the cut accurate on both sides. Accuracy will be easier to achieve if you rotate the block in the vise so that you are always cutting vertically.

9. Fit the blocks onto the pillar. File the centers at a slight angle to approximate the angle on the pillar. This makes fitting easier and reduces the chances of splintering on the back side, because the file does not make contact there. I use an 8-in. or 10-in. double-cut bastard file to start, and then finish with my 6-in. double-cut smooth file.

Check the fit by sliding the pillar into the hole. The block should slide just past the pencil line (drawn in step 8 of the pillar section on p. 66). It probably won't fit at first try, so check where it is contacting and file the offending spot. You should also check the block's squareness to the pillar, rotating it 90 degrees to ensure that it fits the pillar from both directions.

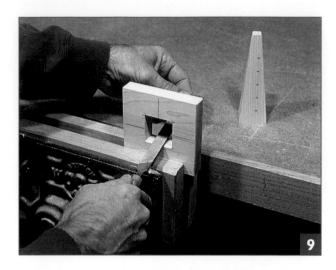

Continue to do this until the block slides just past the layout line on the pillar—between ¹⁄₁₆ in. and ⅛ in. past the line is ideal. Reverse the block, and file this side until the block fits well from either side.

10. File a small bevel onto all the edges of the hole, just to break the sharp corner.

Assembly

To join the base and pillar, glue the two parts together and then install a dowel to strengthen the joint.

1. Glue the pillar to the base. Put glue on the bottom of the pillar, locate it in place, and measure to check that it is centered. Press the pillar down firmly, moving it about ¹⁄₁₆ in. side to side to squeeze out any excess glue. Put a weight on top to hold it firmly. I put a couple of the small blocks in place to provide a platform, and then stick something heavy on top.

2. After the glue is hard, mark center on the bottom of the base, for the location of the dowel.

3. Drill the hole for the dowel. I use a ¾-in. Forstner-style bit, and I clamp the work to the drill-press table.

4. Check that the dowel fits. Dowels are often slightly oversize, so sand the dowel a little if the fit is tight. When it fits, slide the dowel into place and mark the depth of the hole. Cut the dowel to length, allowing it to be ¹⁄₃₂ in. to ¹⁄₁₆ in. longer than the hole depth.

5. Put some glue in the hole, but use it sparingly so that it does not collect and keep the dowel from bottoming out. Tap the dowel into place, leaving it protruding a little.

6. When the glue is hard, sand off the excess dowel.

Finishing

Finish as desired. I find that a salad-bowl finish is best, because young children are likely to enjoy chewing on it a little. Whatever finish you decide to use, check that it is nontoxic. One note of caution: If you do a beautiful multicoat finish, you will likely find the thicker finish causes the blocks to fit differently or to stick. Regardless of the type of finish, you may want to wax the pillar lightly to ensure the blocks slide easily. Again, check that the wax is nontoxic; natural beeswax is a good choice.

Learning through *Play*

THE STACKING PYRAMID is designed for young children, from about one to three years old. It develops fine-motor skills as the shaped blocks are fitted onto the pillar. Children also learn patterning basics as they see the alternating or repeating colors of the blocks. They also begin to differentiate between the sizes of the blocks and learn concepts such as "smaller," "larger," "above," and "below."

As your toddler plays with the Stacking Pyramid, describe the difference in sizes, explaining that some blocks are larger than others and that the largest ones go on first and the smaller ones go on last. Point out the color pattern as well.

Let the child be free and creative, too. The blocks can be stacked without the stand. They can be placed on edge. The holes in the centers can be windows or doors. Stack them from smallest to largest, making an inverted pyramid. The first time my son used this toy, he first put the smallest block on the pillar and built the pyramid inverted on the top. Many times the unexpected provides a teachable moment.

The Ultimate Building Block Set

*e**ducational toy research** continually comes back to building blocks. Durable, safe, and battery free, blocks help children reach a broad range of educational and developmental goals.

In addition, and perhaps most important to the continuing success of these toys, children love to play with blocks. The USA Toy Library Association recently conducted a survey of toy libraries and listed manipulative blocks as one of the most popular toys in the United States, second only to ride-on vehicles. Even adults find it hard to resist sitting on the floor to build a better, taller tower—or to see if it falls when a certain block is removed.

The blocks in this project take a little while to make, mostly because there are so many. But the project is not complex. Whatever difficulty there is comes in making all the cuts and surfaces square and in having clean cuts with very little splintering on the corners. Once the machines are set up carefully (and with sharp blades!), the rest is reasonably easy.

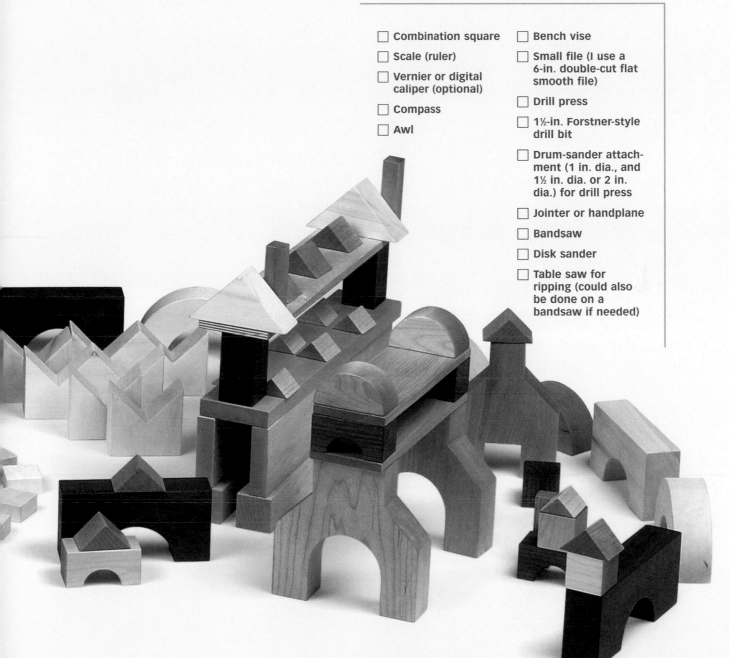

Tools You Need

- ☐ Combination square
- ☐ Scale (ruler)
- ☐ Vernier or digital caliper (optional)
- ☐ Compass
- ☐ Awl

- ☐ Bench vise
- ☐ Small file (I use a 6-in. double-cut flat smooth file)
- ☐ Drill press
- ☐ 1½-in. Forstner-style drill bit
- ☐ Drum-sander attachment (1 in. dia., and 1½ in. dia. or 2 in. dia.) for drill press
- ☐ Jointer or handplane
- ☐ Bandsaw
- ☐ Disk sander
- ☐ Table saw for ripping (could also be done on a bandsaw if needed)

ULTIMATE BUILDING BLOCK SET CUT LIST

BLOCK	SHAPE	THICKNESS	WIDTH	LENGTH	NO. REQ'D.
A-1	Cube	1½ in.	1½ in.	1½ in.	20
A-2	Rectangle	1½ in.	1½ in.	3 in.	12
A-3	Rectangle	1½ in.	1½ in.	4½ in.	6
A-4	Rectangle	1½ in.	1½ in.	6 in.	4
A-5	Rectangle	1½ in.	1½ in.	7½ in.	4
A-6	Rectangle	1½ in.	1½ in.	9 in.	4
A-7	Rectangle	1½ in.	1½ in.	10½ in.	2
A-8	Rectangle	1½ in.	1½ in.	12 in.	2
A-9	Rectangle	1½ in.	1½ in.	13½ in.	2
A-10	Rectangle	1½ in.	1½ in.	15 in.	2
B-1	Rectangle	1½ in.	3 in.	3 in.	4
B-2	Rectangle	1½ in.	3 in.	6 in.	2
B-3	Rectangle	1½ in.	3 in.	9 in.	2
B-4	Rectangle	1½ in.	3 in.	12 in.	2
C-1	Rectangle	¾ in.	3 in.	3 in.	4
C-2	Rectangle	¾ in.	3 in.	6 in.	2
C-3	Rectangle	¾ in.	3 in.	9 in.	2
C-4	Rectangle	¾ in.	3 in.	12 in.	2
C-5	Rectangle	¾ in.	3 in.	15 in.	2
D-1	Rectangle	¾ in.	1½ in.	1½ in.	12
D-2	Rectangle	¾ in.	1½ in.	3 in.	6
D-3	Rectangle	¾ in.	1½ in.	4½ in.	2
D-4	Rectangle	¾ in.	1½ in.	6 in.	2
E-1	Rectangle	⅜ in.	1½ in.	3 in.	4
E-2	Rectangle	⅜ in.	1½ in.	6 in.	2
E-3	Rectangle	⅜ in.	1½ in.	9 in.	2
E-4	Rectangle	⅜ in.	1½ in.	12 in.	2
E-5	Rectangle	⅜ in.	1½ in.	15 in.	2
F-1	Rectangle	⅜ in.	3 in.	3 in.	4
F-2	Rectangle	⅜ in.	3 in.	6 in.	2
F-3	Rectangle	⅜ in.	3 in.	9 in.	2
F-4	Rectangle	⅜ in.	3 in.	12 in.	2
F-5	Rectangle	⅜ in.	3 in.	15 in.	2
G-1	Rectangle	¾ in.	¾ in.	3 in.	12

BLOCK	SHAPE	THICKNESS	WIDTH	LENGTH	NO. REQ'D.
H-1	Quarter Cube	¾ in.	1½ in.	1½ in.	12
H-2	Half cube	1¹⁄₁₆ in.	2⅛ in.	1½ in.	10
H-3	House	1½ in.	3 in.	3 in.	2
H-4	Small crown	1½ in.	3 in.	3 in.	4
H-5	Big crown	1½ in.	3 in.	6 in.	2
H-6	3-in. triangle	1½ in.	2⅛ in.	4¼ in.	2
H-7	6-in. triangle	1½ in.	4¼ in.	8½ in.	2
I-1	Rectangular arch	1½ in.	1½ in.	3 in.	6
I-2	Rectangular arch	1½ in.	3 in.	6 in.	4
I-3	Rounded arch	1½ in.	3 in.	6 in.	4
I-4	Rectangular arch	½ in.	3 in.	7½ in.	2
I-5	Rounded arch	1½ in.	6 in.	12 in.	2
J-1	Arc	1½ in.	¾ in.	1½ in.	4
J-2	Arc	1½ in.	1½ in.	3 in.	4
J-3	Arc	1½ in.	2¼ in.	4½ in.	2
J-4	Arc	1½ in.	3 in.	6 in.	2
K-1	Tower	1½ in.	4½ in.	6 in.	2
K-2	Tower	1½ in.	4½ in.	9 in.	2
K-3	Tower	1½ in.	6 in.	6 in.	2
K-4	Tower	1½ in.	6 in.	9 in.	2
K-5	Tower	1½ in.	6 in.	12 in.	2
L-1	Cylinder	1½ in.	1½ in.	3 in.	2
L-2	Cylinder	1½ in.	1½ in.	6 in.	2
L-3	Cylinder	1½ in.	1½ in.	9 in.	2

Choice of Wood

Hard Eastern maple is my first choice for blocks, but with the total amount of wood nearing 25 bd. ft., cost becomes a major factor. The most practical approach to this project is to use up the small ends of wood left over from other projects. This also has the advantage of producing blocks of different colors for interest and variety.

Don't rule out less expensive, softer woods such as pine or fir. Fir is a good option because, although it is a softwood, it is still quite hard and gets harder with time (if you have ever tried to hammer a nail in an old fir floor joist, you'll know what I mean). Pine will dent, but it is light and readily available in 1½-in. thickness—the basic unit measurement for this block set—in the form of construction lumber.

I used a variety of hardwood (birch, walnut, maple, and aspen) for this set, with fir for some of the larger pieces. You, of course, should pick the wood that best suits your needs.

Overview of Design

There are a few practical considerations when making this block set. Friedrich Froebel, a German educator who, in the 19th century, revolutionized the concepts of learning through play (as well as developing the concept of kindergarten), used blocks extensively in his teaching methods. His sets were all based on a unit block of one cubic inch. Some blocks were 2 in., 3 in., and up to 12 in. long, some were ½ in. wide, and some were triangles, but all sizes were based on the original unit. This allowed the blocks to be used for open-ended creative play as well as to teach the concepts of simple fractions (two half-unit blocks stack to the same height as one full-unit block), addition, subtraction, and even multiplication.

Unit Selection

Some unit blocks sold today are based on a unit size of 1⅜ in., some 1½ in., and others 2 in. Each manufacturer cautions against using other sizes, which are not the "real" standard. In the end, the exact size of the unit is not all that important, so long as all the blocks are based on that unit. I have decided on 1½ in. for a few reasons. First, the original 1-in. unit is a bit small for very young children, both in terms of refined motor skills and as a possible choking hazard. Second, planed 1½-in.-thick wood is easy and inexpensive to come by in the form of lumber. And, third, ½-in. unit increments are quite easy to work with.

It is important to keep all the block sizes consistent and the surfaces square to each other. If the blocks are inaccurate, they not only become less effective as building tools but also less effective as teaching tools. For example, four of the half-unit blocks should stack up to equal two full-unit blocks. If the stacks are noticeably unequal, children will lose the natural learning and understanding of the relationship between sizes and, thus, fractions.

Block Types

There are seven types of blocks included in this set. They are coded on the cut list (see p. 74) with a letter and number for easy reference:

- 1½-in.-square cross section, in lengths varying from 1½ in. long (one unit) to 15 in. long (10 units)

- 1½ in. thick by 3 in. wide, in lengths from 3 in. to 12 in. (two units to 10 units)

- ¾ in. thick by 1½ in. wide (thickness half the width), in lengths from 1½ in. to 6 in. (one unit to four units)

- ¾ in. thick by 3 in. wide, in lengths from 3 in. to 15 in. in 3-in. increments (two units to 10 units)

- 1½-in. cylindrical blocks, in lengths from 3 in. to 9 in. (two, four, and six units)

- triangular blocks of various sizes, from one unit to six units long

- arches and pillars, which are curved or angled pieces of various shapes

Some of the larger pieces have holes drilled in them so the round blocks can be inserted, which allows a whole new type of structural option; hole sizes and spacing are based on the 1½-in. unit.

Making the Blocks

The overall project plan is as follows: First, find or plane all the wood you need. Second, cut strips of the widths you are using. Third, cut these strips to length. And, fourth, cut the arches, arcs, and angles, and drill the holes.

Preparing the Stock

The complete block set requires about 13 sq. ft. (or about 19 bd. ft.) of 1½-in.-thick wood. However, this is the finished amount; to allow for saw cuts and a bit of waste, you need to prepare almost 15 sq. ft. total (or 22½ board ft.). The finished amount of the ¾-in.-thick wood is about 3 sq. ft. (2¼ board ft.). For this project, I collected 4 sq. ft. of ¾-in. stock, mostly scraps that I had on hand.

You may need to laminate to get the 6-in.-wide blocks. You need a total length of 90 in. of 6-in.-wide wood.

For the cylindrical blocks, you need at least 48 in. of 1½-in.-dia. dowel. Dowel usually comes in 36-in. lengths, so get two. Other projects in this book require short pieces, so the extra will likely come in handy.

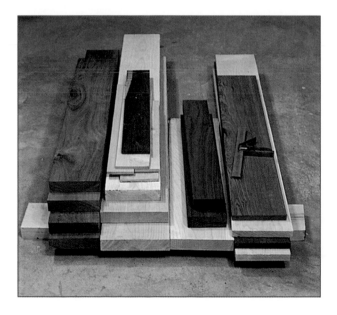

Finally, you need a little bit of ⅜-in.-thick wood. You can plane this down from thicker material or use Baltic birch plywood, which commonly comes in this thickness. Three sq. ft. should be adequate, as the required finished amount is just over 2 sq. ft. Birch plywood is strong and durable, and I have used a few pieces in this set despite the fact that it is not quite as nice in appearance as solid wood.

Cutting the Wide Strips

The 4½-in.- and 6-in.-wide strips will form the I-4 arches, the K-1 to K-5 towers, and the H-6 and H-7 triangles.

1. Cut about 90 in. of 1½-in.-thick by 6-in.-wide stock (finished required length plus saw cuts totals about 80 in.).

2. Cut about 55 inches of 1½-in.-thick by 4½-in.-wide stock (finished required length plus saw cuts totals about 47 in.). This will include the 4¼-in.-wide wood needed for the H-7 triangles.

Cutting the Medium Strips

The 3-in.-wide strips are for all the B blocks, plus the I-2 and I-3 arches, the H-3 houses, the H-4 and H-5 crowns, and the J-4 arcs.

1. Cut about 210 in. of 1½-in.-thick by 3-in.-wide stock (finished required length plus saw cuts totals about 196 in.). This will include the 2⅛-in.-wide wood needed for the H-6 triangles.

2. Cut about 110 in. to 120 in. of ¾-in.-thick by 3-in.-wide stock (finished required length plus saw cuts totals 98 in.) and the same amount of ⅜-in.-thick by 3-in.-wide stock.

Cutting the Narrow Strips

The 1⅞-in.-wide wood will be used to make H-1 quarter cubes and the H-2 half cubes. The 1½-in.-wide wood will be used to make all the A and D blocks, the I-1 arches, and the J-2 arcs.

Ideally, you can joint an edge of your wide stock, saw a 1½-in.-wide strip, and then joint the edge of the stock again before sawing the next 1½-in.-wide strip. This way each strip has a true, jointed edge and only one sawn edge. However, this work can be done quite nicely without either a jointer or planer.

Cut the strips a little oversize to allow for planing later. If you have a thickness planer, leave about ¹⁄₁₆ in. for planing, but if you are using a handplane, then leave only about ¹⁄₃₂ in. One or two light passes with a handplane are sufficient to remove the saw-cut marks, and it is easier to keep the material square if the amount of planing is minimal.

Ensure that the sawblade is set exactly square to the table.

1. Rip a short piece just over 1⅞ in. wide and about 16 in. long for the quarter cubes and half cubes (H-1 and H-2). You will need only about 13 in. of length for all these blocks, but a little extra won't hurt and will make it easier to hold the wood when cross cutting the last few pieces to length later.

2. Cut the 1½-in.-thick by 1½-in.-wide stock. This stock will provide material for all the A blocks, plus I-1 and J-2. The total length required is about 323 in., so cut about 350 in. of total length.

3. Rip the ¾-in.-thick by 1½-in.-wide stock (D-1 to D-4). You will need at least 82 in. including cuts, so prepare about 90 in. of stock.

Cutting the Square Stock

Rip about 45 in. of ¾-in. by ¾-in. stock (needed for G-1) because you will need at least 37½ in. of stock including cuts.

Planing the Sawn Edges

Use the jointer or handplane (and thickness planer if you have one) to smooth these surfaces and remove the saw marks (see the photos below). Take care that the dimensions and angles are accurate, so that the square strips actually end up square.

A-1 to A-10 blocks

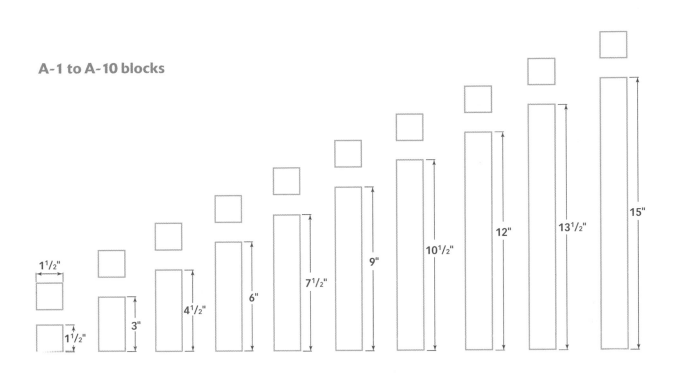

Cutting the Blocks to Length

The drawing above outlines lengths for each block. Here are some production suggestions that might make this process more efficient:

1. Cut the longest blocks first so that the shorter ends can be utilized for cutting the short blocks and cubes at the end.

2. Cut all blocks of a given length at the same time to avoid having to set up the stop blocks again later. For example, cut blocks A-2, B-1, C-1, D-2, E-1, F-1, G-1, H-3, H-4, I-1, and J-2 at the same setting because they are all 3 in. long.

3. Cut the blocks for the arches (I-1 to I-5) and the arcs (J-1 to J-4). The curves can be cut later. Label the I and J blocks so they don't get lost in the clutter.

One way to do accomplish this part of the project is with a miter saw (see the photo top left). Clamp a stop on the saw, which is set to cut the blocks to length (plus ¹⁄₆₄ in. for sanding). You can also do this on the table saw by clamping a stop on the miter gauge (see the photo middle left). A third method involves using the bandsaw (see the photo bottom left). The bandsaw method has several advantages. First, it is safer when cutting the short lengths. Second, it is less likely to chip or splinter the wood as the blade breaks through. Third, the saw cut (kerf) is quite a bit thinner, saving a significant amount of wood when you have many cuts.

Cutting the Triangular and Peaked Blocks

There are several ways to make H-1 and H-2, the quarter cubes and half cubes (triangles), respectively, but in the end the simplest system is to make a rectangular block 1⅞ in. wide by 1½ in. thick by 1½ in. long, then saw it diagonally on the bandsaw. While you could rip a long piece that is triangular in cross section, then cut off 1½-in. lengths, the triangular strips are a little more difficult to rip accurately and also more awkward to hold in a vise for planing or sanding.

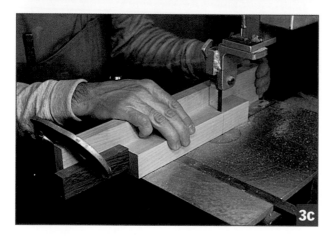

1. Retrieve the piece of 1½-in.-thick wood, which is at least 1⅞ in. wide, that you cut earlier.

2. Cut eight pieces just over 1½ in. long (¹⁄₆₄ in. to ¹⁄₃₂ in. over, to allow for sanding).

3. Sand the ends square and smooth. I use the disk sander (fine-grit disk) with a miter gauge to keep the ends as square as possible.

4. On the end grain of three of the blocks, mark out for the quarter cubes as shown in the drawing (bottom left). Use a 45-degree angle on a combination square, or measure out the dimensions as follows: Draw a centerline lengthways, measure ¾ in. in from each end of the centerline, and join these ¾-in. marks to the corners to produce the 45-degree

CUBES AND HOUSES

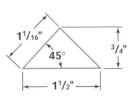

Quarter cube (H-1)

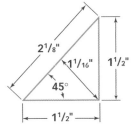

Half cube (H-2)

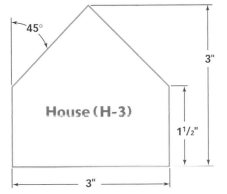

House (H-3)

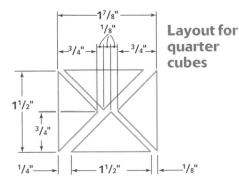

Layout for quarter cubes

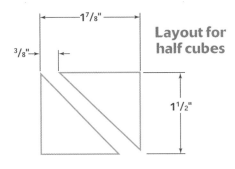

Layout for half cubes

6. Use a bandsaw to cut out all the triangles (10 half cubes and 12 quarter cubes).

7. Use a disk sander to sand to the line. Do this carefully.

8. Check that the ends are square and the corners are 45 degrees.

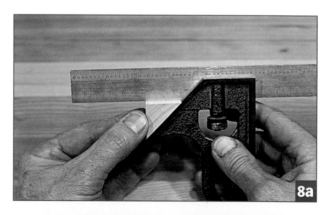

lines. These form the end triangles (see the photo top left).

Measure ⅛ in. over and then 1½ in. over, to lay out the base of the center triangles, as shown in the bottom photo above. The center intersections of these triangles are ⅛ in. from each other and ⅛ in. from the two end triangles.

5. Take the remaining five blocks and lay out the diagonal lines for the half cubes. Measure 1½ in. in on each of the long sides. Join this point with the opposite corner, and you will have the two lines that bracket the saw cut.

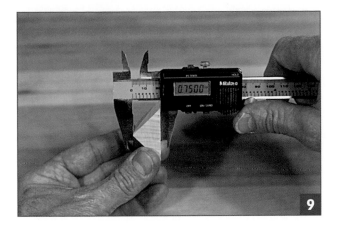

9. For the quarter cubes, make sure the sides are square to each other and to the ends. Measure from the base to the point, which should be ¾ in. (0.75).

For the half cubes, make sure the sides are the same length and the measurement from the base to the point is 1¹⁄₁₆ in. (1.06). Use a caliper (as shown in the photo above left) or a ruler.

10. The blocks H-3 to H-7 can be cut on a band-saw. Lay out on 1½-in.-thick wood. All angles are 45 degrees. Leave ¹⁄₆₄ in. for filing and sanding the angles later, but cut as accurately as possible using the bandsaw. (The photo above right shows H-6 being sawn.)

CROWNS AND TRIANGLES

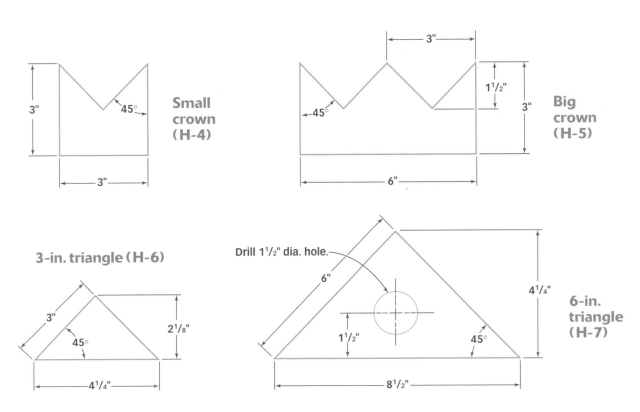

Small crown (H-4)

Big crown (H-5)

3-in. triangle (H-6)

6-in. triangle (H-7)

Drill 1½" dia. hole.

11. File the angles on H-4 and H-6, taking care to keep the surfaces as flat as possible.

12. Disk-sand the angles on H-7, just enough to remove the saw marks.

13. Drill the 1½-in.-dia. hole in H-7. Use a Forstner-style bit if possible. Clamp the part on a backing board to eliminate chipout as the drill breaks through.

14. Sand the hole a little using a drum-sander attachment on the drill press. This both smoothes the hole and enlarges it a bit so that a 1½-in.-dia. dowel will fit easily.

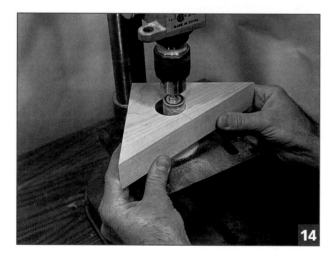

Cutting the Arcs and Arches

1. Collect the I and J blocks that you marked earlier (in step 3 of "Cutting the Blocks to Length" on p. 79).

2. Lay out for the arches and arcs, using a compass (see the drawings right and facing page).

3. Drill the ¾ in. radius in I-1. Use a 1½-in. drill and clamp two blocks together, as shown in the photo left facing page.

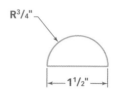

R³/₄"

1½"

1 ½-in. arc (J-1)

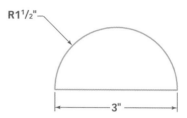

R1½"

3"

3-in. arc (J-2)

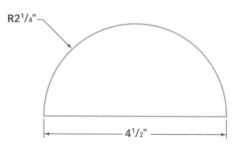

R2¼"

4½"

4½-in. arc (J-3)

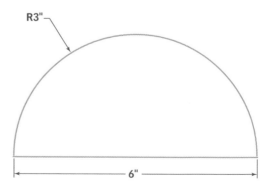

R3"

6"

6-in. arc (J-4)

Small rectangular arch (I-1)

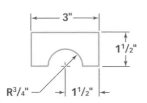

Medium rectangular arch (I-2)

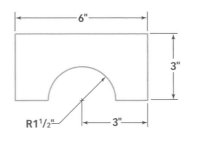

Large rectangular arch (I-4)

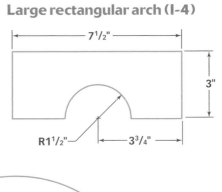

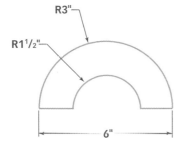

Small rounded arch (I-3)

Large rounded arch (I-5)

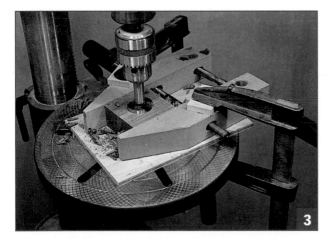

4. Using the bandsaw, saw the curves in arches I-2 and I-3 (allowing ¼ in. to ⅓₂ in. for sanding later).

A ¼-in.-wide blade will allow you to cut the sharp curves, but a few relief cuts are always a good idea.

5. Sand the curves smooth using the drum-sander attachment.

6. Saw out the arcs J-1 to J-4, following a similar process.

7. Sand the inside cuts using a drum sander (as with the arches). Sand the outside contours by hand or by using a disk sander and then finishing by hand.

Cutting the Tower Blocks

1. Lay out for the tower blocks. You can replace the arches in towers K-3, K-4, and K-5 with a straight line if you want them to match K-1 and K-2. Also mark the hole locations now (see the drawings facing page).

2. Drill the 1½ in.-dia. holes. Use a Forstner-type bit as you did with triangle H-7 (see p. 84).

3. Saw to shape, again leaving ⅟₆₄ in. to ⅟₃₂ in. all around to allow for sanding. Cut as accurately as possible.

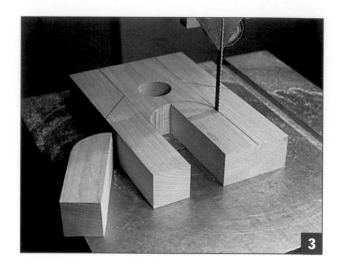

4. File and sand to shape. I use the disk sander where possible, using a fine-grit disk.

5. Sand the inside of the holes, using a drum-sander attachment, as was done for triangle H-7. Sand the curves as well.

Cutting the Cylindrical Blocks

These are lengths of 1½-in.-dia. dowel. For this project, I used maple, the most common dowel. You will need 36 in. of finished length, plus saw cuts (about 37 in. long total). This may mean that you need more than one length of dowel, if you have 36-in.-long pieces. If necessary, cut one or both of the 6-in.-long pieces (L-1) down to 4½ in. long so that you can get all the blocks out of one length.

1. Cut two pieces 3 in. long, two pieces 6 in. long, and two pieces 9 in. long.

2. If you have extra material, you may consider making two more of the longer blocks 9 in. or even 12 in. long.

RECTANGULAR-ARCH TOWERS

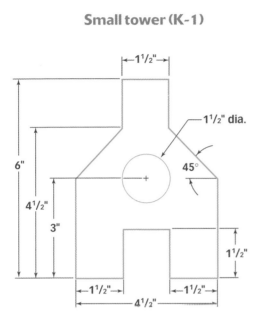

Small tower (K-1)

1¹/₂"
1¹/₂" dia.
45°
6"
4¹/₂"
3"
1¹/₂"
1¹/₂"
1¹/₂"
4¹/₂"

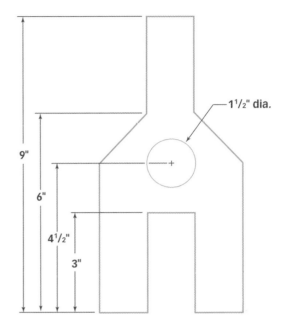

1¹/₂" dia.
9"
6"
4¹/₂"
3"

Large tower (K-2)

ROUNDED-ARCH TOWERS

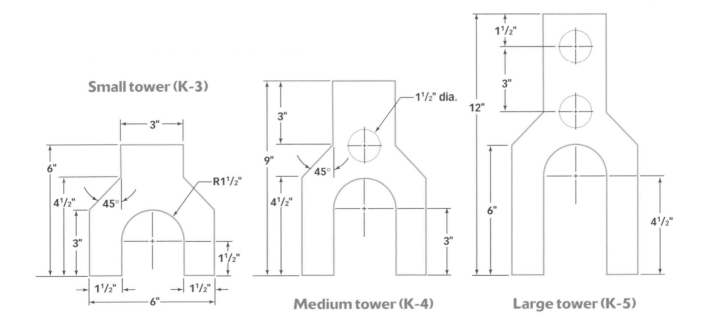

Small tower (K-3)

3"
R1¹/₂"
6"
4¹/₂"
45°
3"
1¹/₂"
1¹/₂"
1¹/₂"
6"

1¹/₂" dia.
3"
9"
45°
4¹/₂"
3"

Medium tower (K-4)

1¹/₂"
3"
12"
6"
4¹/₂"

Large tower (K-5)

Sanding

I sand all the ends of the blocks using a disk sander. There are just too many blocks for me to tackle by hand. The main concern here is to keep the ends square to the rest of the block. Several things can help you with this:

- Make sure that the sander table is square to the disk (or belt, if you are using a belt sander).

- Use a disk that will not remove wood very quickly. A fine-grit disk is a good idea, as is one that is a bit dull—but not so dull as to burn the wood.

- Use a miter gauge on the sander table. Extend the gauge with a piece of wood so it nearly touches the disk, or make a simple nonadjusting 90-degree gauge as shown in the photo top right.

- Press lightly, and visually check often to ensure that you are not taking more off one side than the other. The saw marks should be disappearing evenly over the end, not just in one corner or side. Checking with a square is a good idea as well.

- Rotate the block once or twice so that the same side is not always down. This will help even out any small errors that you may make.

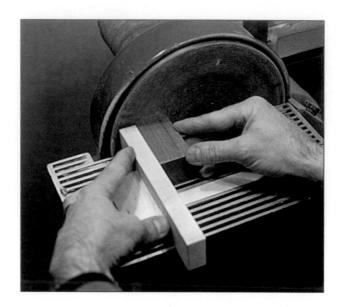

Rounding the Corners

This can be done by hand with sandpaper and a fine file or with a router and a small roundover bit. A ⅛-in. roundover bit is plenty big enough for these blocks. With so many blocks to do, I prefer using a router (as shown in the photo below). Do all the edges, including the edges of the holes.

Finishing

Some purchased wooden blocks are not finished, and leaving this set unfinished makes the process less time-consuming, of course, and allows slight damage to be sanded out. I think this is a reasonable option. However, I have found that unfinished blocks soon became grubby, and they are not water resistant.

I have also tried finishing with a spray urethane, but sanding between coats takes a lot of time, and the final product is a bit slippery for some types of play.

The finish I prefer is a linseed-oil finish called "varnish oil" (see the finishing section on p. 13 and the list of suppliers on p. 130). This finish is surprisingly good after only one coat, and the blocks can be handled to some extent while the finish is still wet. When dry and buffed, the finish looks good, the blocks can be wiped clean with a damp cloth, and they can be refinished easily if needed.

Learning through *Play*

NOT ONLY IS THIS the Ultimate Building Block Set because it has so many different blocks but also because it is one of the best possible educational and developmental toys. There are so many ways in which blocks are educational, but Patricia Gaffney Ansel, working with the Yale-New Haven Teachers Institute, perhaps said it best: They encourage imagination and creativity; contribute to a sense of accomplishment and self-esteem through building; stimulate math and science prenumber skills (i.e., size and shape recognition, matching and classification, and problem solving) and visual discrimination, a prereading skill; help develop language and vocabulary; and refine motor skills and eye-hand coordination.

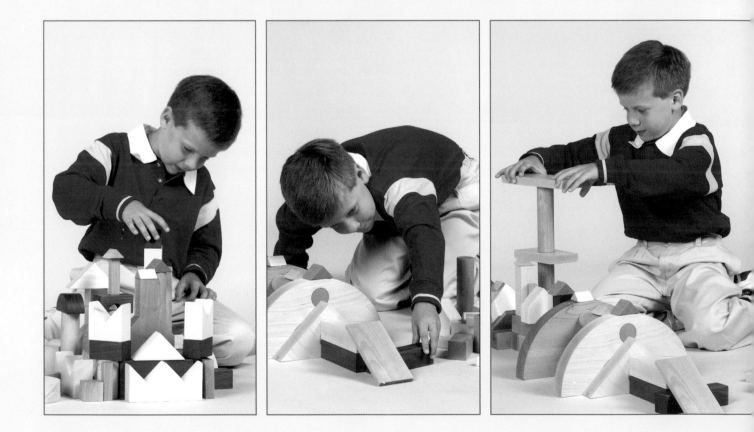

Blocks can be enjoyed by anyone, but they are particularly ideal for children seven months to 12 years old, depending on the type of play. For children younger than seven months, the blocks should be made from a soft material. While the U.S. Consumer Product Safety Commission states that a rounded-edge caution can be lifted for children at 12 months, it makes no sense to risk it—hence the beveled edges in this block set.

Also, spherical shapes (smaller than 1¾ in. dia.) are discouraged because this ball shape can be especially hard to remove from a young child's mouth. While none of the blocks in this set are spherical, it is possible to buy wooden balls to add to the set, so it is worth repeating this caution.

There are nearly as many ways to play with blocks as there are educational opportunities. For open-ended, creative play, try some of the following with your child. Collect photos or drawings of interesting buildings and structures (pyramids, towers, houses, barns, etc.), and encourage the child to draw inspiration from them. Talk about the basic shapes of objects or buildings: Are they long and thin? What shapes make good building blocks? What is the shape of a roof or a window? What is the shape of a chair, a couch, or a cat? Can you stack cats? Why not?

For more specific educational activities, blocks can be used in the following ways:

Classification and sorting.
Blocks can be sorted by length, width, or thickness. Children could sort them into blocks that have curves (arcs) and those with only straight edges. Or, they can be sorted into cubes, rectangles, or other shapes. They can also be sorted by size, smallest to largest.

Introduction to fractions.
Use several small blocks to equal one large one. For example, two cubes together add up to one double-length block, so each cube is one-half the size of the double block. This concept works right up to the longest block, which is 10 cubes (unit blocks) long.

Introduction to decimals.
Use the 10 unit blocks plus the cube blocks to show the concept of decimals. If each cube is 0.1, the 10-unit block is 1.0. Have kids combine these blocks to form various decimals, such as 1.4 (one long block plus four cubes).

Addition and subtraction.
Unit blocks, because of their simple, consistent cube shape, are helpful when explaining addition and subtraction, as well as multiplication and division. Have children use the blocks as manipulatives to show arithmetical functions, such as: If you have two blocks, and I give you three more, how many do you have now?

Vocabulary.
Blocks can be used as manipulatives to show the meaning of words such as "under," "over," and "beside." Place a large block under a small one, and explain the words "under" and "over." Reverse the position of the blocks, and have the child state which block is under and which one is over.

Puzzle Train

*t*rains are a great favorite with kids. They love to load and hook up different train cars and pull them around. This train consists of a traditional steam locomotive combined with a variety of cars. If you don't want to make all six cars to start with, choose the ones that are best suited to the child you have in mind—the remaining cars make great gifts later.

The different cars have various educational goals attached to them, but a few things can be said about the train as a whole. For younger children, fine-motor skills are practiced as cars are hooked up to each other and to the locomotive. Similarly, loading and unloading the cars helps improve eye-hand coordination. Several cars have specific loads that teach basic math concepts, while other cars encourage open-ended play, which helps build imagination and creativity. See the "Learning through Play" sidebar on p. 128 for detailed information about each car's educational value and play suggestions.

No parts of this train are particularly difficult to build. The design of the locomotive and of most of the cars is quite flexible—each part could be a little longer or taller and still work well. When exact sizes are critical, I will bring it to your attention. The locomotive and caboose will take the most time, maybe a day for each by the time each piece is sanded and finished. The other cars are a lot faster.

Tools You Need

- ☐ Awl
- ☐ Scale (ruler)
- ☐ Square
- ☐ Small file (I use a 6-in. double-cut flat smooth file)
- ☐ Clamp suitable to hold wood to drill-press table
- ☐ Three or four parallel clamps (Jorgensen)
- ☐ Handplane
- ☐ Coping saw
- ☐ Mallet

- ☐ Bench vise
- ☐ Drill press
- ☐ 11⁄32-in. and 7⁄32-in. drill bits (for axle pins)
- ☐ ¼-in., "F," ⅜-in., ½-in., 9⁄16-in., and ⅝-in. drill bits
- ☐ Countersink bit
- ☐ ¾-in. drill bit or Forstner-style bit
- ☐ Drill-press vise (optional but handy)
- ☐ Disk/belt sander
- ☐ Bandsaw

LOCOMOTIVE **CUT LIST**

PART NAME	FINISH DIMENSIONS L X W X T	NO. REQ'D.	NOTES
Frame	8⁵⁄₁₆ in. x 1¾ in. x 2½ in.	1	
Boiler	2 in. dia. x 5¾ in.	1	Could use 1½ in. dia. or 1¾ in. dia.
Cab sides	2½ in. x 2⅝ in. x ¼ in.	2	Mirror images
Stack	¼ in. dia. x 1⅜ in.	1	
Dome	⅝ in. dia. x 1¼ in.	1	
Funnel	1⅝ in. dia. x 3¼ in.	1	Factory-made funnel
Cab roof	2¾ in. x 3⅜ in. x ¼ in.	1	Grain runs crossways to train.
Walkways	3 in. x ½ in. x ¼ in.	2	
Small wheels	1 in. dia. x ⅜ in.	2	Factory-made wheels
Large wheels	2 in. dia. x ⅝ in.	4	Factory-made wheels
Small axle pins	⁷⁄₃₂ in. dia.	2	Factory-made standard axle pins
Large axle pins	¹¹⁄₃₂ in. dia.	7	Factory-made standard axle pins (two for piston rods, four for wheels, one for headlight)
Cylinders	¾ in. dia. x 1 in.	2	
Piston rod			See entry for large axle pins.
Coupler dowel	¼ in. dia. x ¾ in.	1	Cut ¹³⁄₁₆ in. long.
Cowcatcher	2⅝ in. x 1³⁄₁₆ in. x 1 in.	1	

Locomotive

The locomotive is the heart of any train, and children seem to find this one particularly appealing. I've refined it over the years in response to their requests and criticisms.

Children really respond to color, and I generally try to incorporate some color using scraps of exotic species. For this locomotive, the maple used in the frame and boiler gets a boost from the purpleheart cab, cowcatcher, and walkways. Other woods such as padauk or yellowheart would work well also. The wheels, axle pins, and stack were purchased at a hobby store and generally come standard in maple. There is nothing stopping you from making these as well, if you have a lathe and the desire to do so.

Frame

This frame is the main block of wood that supports the boiler, cab, and wheels.

1. Cut a block of wood 2½ in. wide, 1¾ in. thick, and 8⁵⁄₁₆ in. long, keeping all surfaces as straight and square as possible. If you don't have wood that is thick enough, you could laminate or even use 1½-in.-thick wood instead.

2. Lay out the side profile, and mark the location of the holes with an awl. The axle holes can be drilled right through, so lay out on one side only. If you have wood with a dramatic grain, you may want to drill from each side as the drill bit may wander a bit.

LOCOMOTIVE PLAN

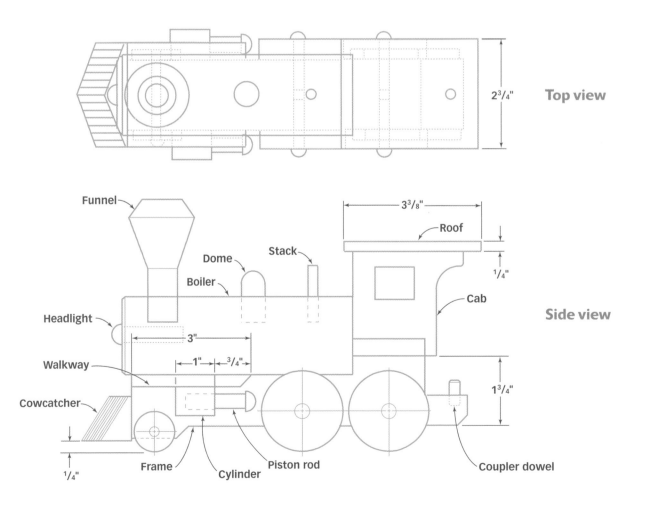

Top view

2³⁄₄"

Funnel
Dome
Stack
Boiler
Headlight
Walkway
Cowcatcher
Frame
Cylinder
Piston rod
Coupler dowel
Roof
Cab

Side view

3³⁄₈"
¹⁄₄"
3"
1"
³⁄₄"
1³⁄₄"
¹⁄₄"

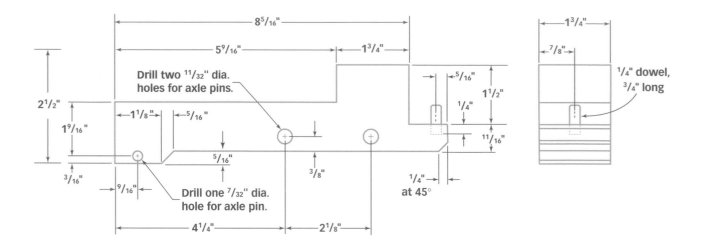

Drill two ¹¹/₃₂" dia. holes for axle pins.

Drill one ⁷/₃₂" dia. hole for axle pin.

8⁵/₁₆"

5⁹/₁₆"

1³/₄"

1³/₄"

⁷/₈"

¼" dowel, ¾" long

2½"

1⁹/₁₆"

1¹/₈"

⁵/₁₆"

⁵/₁₆"

1½"

¼"

¹¹/₁₆"

³/₁₆"

⁹/₁₆"

⁵/₁₆"

³/₈"

¼"
at 45°

4¼"

2¹/₈"

Check that all six wheels will contact on a flat surface. The center of the large wheel is ½ in. above the center of the small wheel. If your wheels are not 1 in. dia. and 2 in. dia., you may need to adjust the center of the holes accordingly.

3. Saw to shape using a bandsaw. Cut as accurately as possible to minimize filing and sanding later.

4. File and sand the ends square. I use a miter gauge when using the disk sander, which works well as long as the disk is fine grit. In places where a disk sander is not an

3

option, I tend to use sandpaper and a small smooth file, which works quite well on end grain.

5. To drill the axle holes, clamp the frame to the drill-press table with a wood scrap under the frame to reduce any splintering as the drill breaks through.

Drill the axle holes to fit your axle pins—generally ¹¹/₃₂ in. dia. Don't install the wheels yet; the locomotive is easier to work with if the wheels are left off until the end.

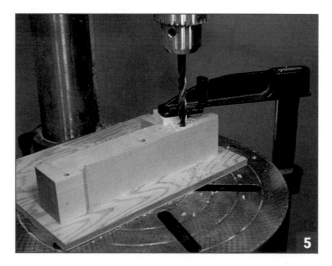

5

6. Lay out and drill the coupler hole. It should be sized to fit your ¼-in.-dia. dowel. Dowels are often slightly oversize, so check the sizing to ensure that the wood doesn't split as the dowel is tapped in. Alternately, the dowel can be sanded a little in the drill press.

7. Cut the coupler dowel to rough length (about ¹¹/₁₆ in.). Sand and bevel one end.

8. Put a little glue in the coupler hole and tap the dowel into place.

9. When the glue is hard, sand the bottom of the dowel flush with the bottom of the locomotive.

Boiler

The boiler is made from 2-in.-dia. dowel. I have also used slightly smaller-diameter dowel, but the larger size looks a little better in my opinion. You could also make this part on a lathe if you wanted to.

The bottom of the boiler is flattened slightly to provide a glue surface, and the top requires three holes—for the smokestack, whistle, and housing—the exact location of which is not important. The funnel that simulates the smokestack is inexpensive and widely available at hobby stores—or, again, if you have a lathe and the inclination, this part can be quickly made.

1. Cut the 2-in.-dia. dowel to length.

2. Plane or sand (using a belt sander) the flat on the bottom of the boiler. The exact width of the flat doesn't matter, but shoot for ¾ in. wide, making sure the width is even along the length of the part.

BOILER DETAILS

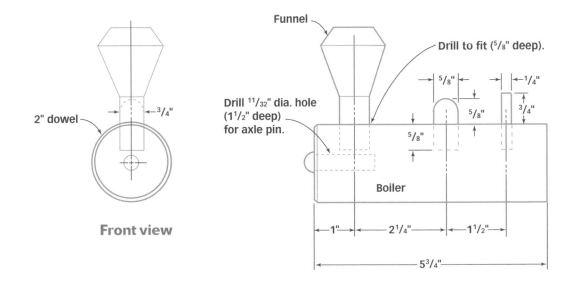

Funnel

Drill to fit (⁵/₈" deep).

⁵/₈"

¹/₄"

³/₄"

⁵/₈"

⁵/₈"

2" dowel

³/₄"

Drill ¹¹/₃₂" dia. hole
(1¹/₂" deep)
for axle pin.

Front view

Boiler

1"

2¹/₄"

1¹/₂"

5³/₄"

Side view

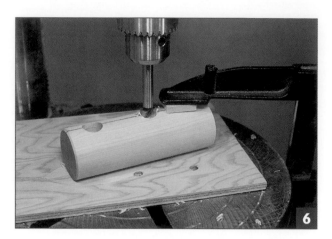

3. Sand the ends, making sure they are square to the sides. Check that one end fits into the notch on the locomotive frame. If you need to adjust the angle on the boiler, do so now.

4. Bevel the front end slightly.

5. Lay out for the holes on the top. On old locomotives, the smokestack, whistle, and housings (domes) that contained regulator and safety valves were mounted to the top of the boiler. These holes are for the dowels that will simulate those parts.

Hole size is not critical; if you don't have a ⅝-in. bit or dowel, just use ½ in. or whatever size is convenient. The size of the hole for the funnel, however, depends on the size of the funnel itself (commonly ¾ in. dia.).

To do the layout, find the center of each end and draw a vertical line up to the top. Join these end lines with a line along the top.

6. Clamp the boiler in a vise or with a clamp as shown, and drill the holes.

7. Drill the hole in the end for the headlight (the head of an axle pin—see the cut list). This hole will generally be ¹¹⁄₃₂ in. dia. because that tends to be the standard diameter of factory-made axle pins. If your axle pins are a different diameter, simply adjust accordingly.

8. When the boiler is sanded and fits well onto the frame, glue it in place.

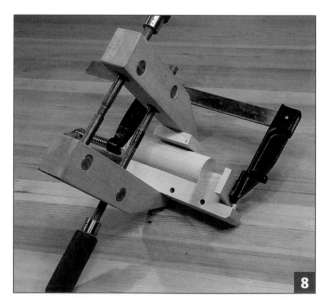

9. Cut a 1¼-in. piece of ¼-in.-dia. dowel. Sand the ends and bevel one end.

10. Before cutting the ⅝-in.-dia. dowel to length, round one end. I use the disk sander and then hand-sand the end smooth.

11. Cut the ⅝-in.-dia. dowel 1¼ in. long.

12. Use a toothpick to put a little glue in each of the holes, and install the ¼-in.-dia. dowel, the dome, the funnel, and the headlight axle pin.

Cab

This simple cab is made up of two sides and a roof. The end of the boiler doubles as the front of the cab. When the sides are attached to the locomotive, the grain should run vertically. Cut out the windows before sawing the parts to size. This will make it a little easier to hold while drilling and sawing.

1. Use a piece of ¼-in.-thick wood, at least 2⅝ in. wide and at least 5⅛ in. long.

2. Lay out for the outline as well as the windows. Don't forget that there are left and right sides.

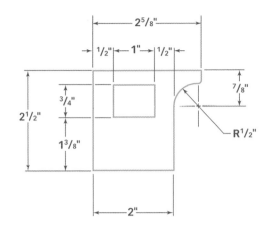

3. Lay out for the ¼-in.-dia. holes at the corners of the windows by measuring ⅛ in. in from each corner and marking the intersection with an awl.

4. Drill the holes. Have the wood clamped on a scrap piece to reduce splintering as the drill breaks through. Keep the hole locations as accurate as possible.

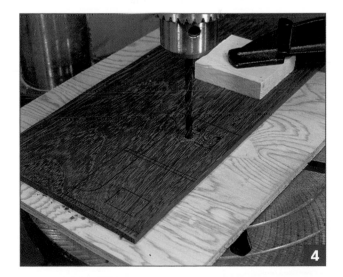

5. Use a coping saw to cut out the window. This will splinter the wood slightly, so you'll probably want to designate the layout side as the inside of the car. If for any reason you decide to make the layout side the outside of the car, then redo the layout  on the other side, making sure you join up the edges of the holes.

6. File the edges of the window with a small smooth file, squaring off the corners. Bevel the sharp edges slightly.

7. Bandsaw the outside contours.

8. File and sand the edges as needed. To finish the rounded corner, I use a small drum-sander attachment on a drill press. Sand the inside surfaces before assembly.

The top edges do not need final sanding now because the roof goes on here later. They will be sanded after gluing, to ensure that both surfaces are aligned.

9. Locate the sides on the frame by marking two tiny dots 1¼ in. up from the bottom on both sides of the frame.

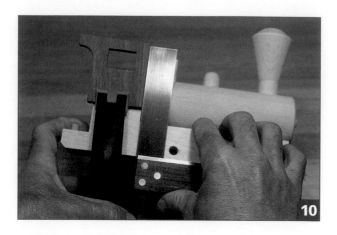

10. Glue the sides in place one at a time. The bottom of the sides should just cover the two layout dots. The front edge contacts the back of the boiler, and the back edge should be square to the frame.

11. Glue the second side in place. The top edges should be even when checked with a square.

12. Sand the top edges flat and even. This can be done carefully using a miter gauge and a disk sander, or it can be done by hand using a flat board with a piece of coarse sandpaper attached.

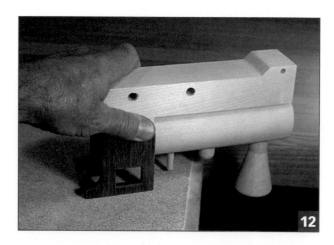

13. Saw the roof to size. For strength reasons, the grain should be crossways to the locomotive.

14. Sand and bevel the edges to remove all sharp corners. Sand all surfaces of the roof, as well as the cab sides, prior to assembly.

15. Apply glue to the tops of the cab sides, and put the roof in place. Placing a weight on top of the roof provides simple clamping pressure.

16. Remove excess glue.

17. To reinforce the end-grain joint, make gussets. Cut two strips of ¼-in.-thick wood ¼ in. wide by 2¼ in. long.

18. Bevel one corner, if desired, for appearance.

19. Put glue on two sides of the gusset, and install by rubbing back and forth slightly to spread the glue evenly. There is no need to clamp.

Walkways

These walkways are simple simulations of the guards and walkways that traditional locomotives often had. Ours are small strips of wood glued to each side. Though a simple detail, they lend a bit of charm to our toy engine.

1. Cut two strips of wood ¼ in. thick by ½ in. wide by 3 in. long.

2. Saw or sand a 45-degree bevel on one end. The exact angle does not matter.

3. Sand and bevel all corners, except the surface where the walkway attaches to the frame.

4. Apply glue to the inside surface of the walkway, and press it into place. Locating the walkway about ¹⁄₁₆ in. below the top surface of the frame reduces alignment difficulties.

Wheel Assembly

At this point, the wheels should be installed. I use factory-made maple axle pins, with an ¹¹⁄₃₂ in. dia. These are intended to fit a ⅜-in.-dia. hole in the wheel and are inexpensive. If you have a lathe, these could be turned nicely and would look sharp made from a wood with dramatic color.

1. Place the wheels and axle pins in place, but don't glue them yet. The pins just need to be pushed in ½ in. or so. Slide the wheels close to the frame and check that all the wheels turn when the locomotive is pushed along a flat surface. If one of the wheels doesn't contact the floor surface because of some small inaccuracy, just drill the wheel-hole center out a little (¹⁄₆₄ in. oversize will likely do it, although it could require up to ¹⁄₃₂ in). The enlarged hole will now allow the wheel to contact the floor, enabling the offending wheel to spin with the rest. For some kids—including one of mine—this feature is important.

2. When the wheels fit to your satisfaction, put a little paraffin wax on the pin but only on the section that will contact the wheel. The wax acts as a lubricant, making the wheels spin noticeably easier. The end to be glued must remain clean. Alternatively, it is sometimes easier to put a little paste wax into the wheel with a Q-tip®.

3. Use a toothpick to put glue in the holes in the locomotive and then tap the axle pins into place. Don't make them too tight—a little loose is a better alternative. If the pin is too tight against the wheel, the wheel can't spin. And, since the pin is hard to pull back out (I've tried), you will end up drilling the pin out and trying again.

Cylinder and Piston Rod

The cylinder is a short length of ¾-in.-dia. dowel, and the piston rod is just another axle pin. To my surprise, one of the first comments regarding the original train I created was from a child who felt the cylinder and piston rod were the best parts of the locomotive, so I have dutifully included this simple mechanism on every locomotive since.

1. Cut the dowel to length.

2. Sand the ends and bevel the corners slightly.

3. Drill the hole in the end to fit the axle pin (generally ¹¹⁄₃₂ in. dia.).

4. Sand a small flat (about ¼ in. wide) along the side of the cylinder to provide a gluing surface.

5. Put some glue in the hole, and install the axle pin. It should protrude about 1 in.

6. Glue the cylinder/piston assembly in place. A gap of ⅛ in. to ¼ in. works best. The cylinder should contact the walkway as well.

Cowcatcher

The cowcatcher needs to be fairly sturdy because it is often called upon to act as a crash bumper. Saw it out of a small block of wood, and glue it directly to the front of the locomotive.

1. Saw out a block 1 in. thick, at least 1¼ in. wide, and at least 2⅝ in. long. Ideally the block should start off at least 4 in. long to make sawing the angles safer. It can be cut down to 2⅝ in. long after all the angle work is done.

2. Lay out for the triangular shape on the top surface.

3. Set the bandsaw table to 60 degrees.

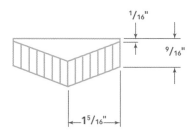

1/16"

9/16"

1⁵/₁₆"

Top view

2⁵/₈"

1"

Front view

9/16"

1/16"

30°

9/16"

1³/₁₆"

Side view

6

very little clamping pressure; the joint will actually be very strong, even on the end grain of the frame. Ensure that the cowcatcher is centered and level before the glue starts to set up.

4

4. Saw to the lines.

5. File or sand the cut edges until they're smooth.

6. Glue the cowcatcher to the front of the frame. There's no good way to clamp this, but the glue surface is quite large so just apply the glue to the front of the frame and press the cowcatcher in place. Work the cowcatcher back and forth slightly to squeeze out excess glue, and let it harden. White carpenters glue (polyvinyl acetate, or PVA) needs

Domed Cap (optional)

If you like the appearance of a domed cap on the locomotive's small stack, just put a dowel cap on it (as shown in the photo above; an extra cap is resting on the car's roof to show the underside). These small caps can be purchased at hobby or woodworking stores.

Car Frames

The drawings and instructions accommodate six cars, but you don't need to make all of them at once. You may decide to make three or four cars and then add more later. You may also want to create some of your own designs, making different or additional cars. However, the frames—or bases—are all the same. I make all the frames first and then add various structures to each one. The frames in these photos are made from maple.

TRAIN-CAR FRAME PLAN

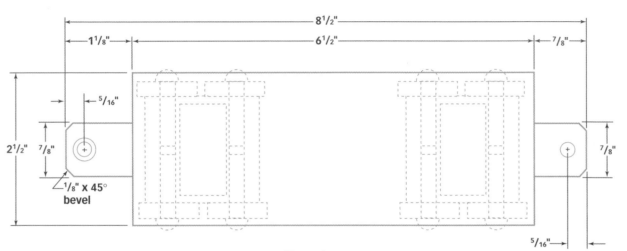

Top view

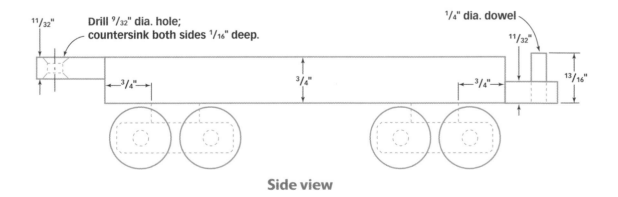

Side view

PART NAME	FINISH DIMENSIONS L X W X T	NO. REQ'D.	NOTES
Frame	8½ in. x 2½ in. x ¾ in.	1	
Axle housings	1⅞ in. x 1¾ in. x ½ in.	2	
Axle-housing spacers	1½ in. x ¾ in. x ⁵⁄₁₆ in.	2	
Wheels	1 in. dia. x ⅜ in.	8	Factory-made wheels
Axle pins	⁷⁄₃₂ in. dia.	8	Factory-made standard pins
Coupler dowel	¼ in. dia. x ¹³⁄₁₆ in.	1	Cut ⅞ in.; trim later.

1. Prepare 2½-in.-wide by ¾-in.-thick wood. You will need at least 8⅝ in. of length for each car frame, including saw cuts. In total, this is at least 52 in. of wood if you are making all six cars at once.

2. Cut the frames to length, making sure the ends are square to the edges.

3. Lay out for the coupler tabs at each end. On one side, draw the top view, and on one edge, carry the lines over and draw the center cut line.

4. Make the cuts in from the ends, freehand. It is possible to set up stops on the table saw and use it to make these cuts, but after trying a few methods of mass production, I found that the quickest and simplest method was to use the bandsaw.

The coupling tabs can vary a little in size and still work perfectly. If you saw close to the line and end your cuts consistently close to the stop line, the filing and sanding work will be much easier.

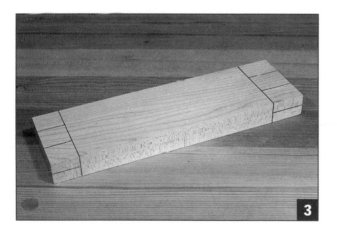

5. Set up a fence for cutting the centerlines on the edge of the tabs. Cut down the center of the line, because the tabs should be a little less than half the width of the frame. This will allow a small gap between the tabs when the cars are coupled together. If there is no gap, it is more likely that the tabs will carry the weight, and the wheels may end up off the ground.

Make sure the face of the fence is square to the table, and the blade of the saw is also square to the table (parallel to the fence's face). The fence on my shopmade bandsaw is just a hardwood board, which works fine.

6. Saw to the perpendicular line (¾ in. from one end, 1⅛ in. from the other).

7. Use a miter gauge to make the vertical crosscut. Again, cut close to the line, being very careful to keep the cut straight and to end it just before the stop line.

8. Trim out the corners. Use the existing cut as a reference line, sawing as close as you can to that cut without touching it. Sawing about ¼4 in. away from the line is ideal, leaving only this small amount to remove with a file and sandpaper.

9. Use a small smooth file (I have a 6-in. double-cut smooth file that works well) to remove the saw marks and even out the small steps that remain after sawing.

10. Lay out for the holes in the tabs, and mark the hole locations with an awl or other sharp tool.

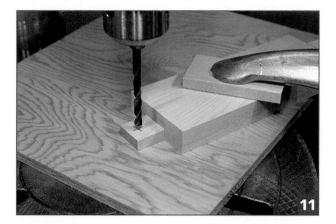

11. Drill the hole in the smaller tab so that it is a tight fit on ¼-in.-dia. dowel. This hole may need to be a bit larger than ¼ in. dia., depending on the exact size of your dowel. I generally use an "F" bit, which is slightly larger than ¼ in., or a ¹⁷/₆₄-in. bit, which is a little larger still. Try out your bit size on a small scrap to ensure that the dowel will not split the tab when installed later.

12. Drill the hole in the larger tab a little oversize (⁹/₃₂ in. dia.), which allows a little clearance on the ¼-in.-dia. coupling dowel. Countersink each side. This allows the cars to be coupled together more easily, as well as allowing the car to pivot up and down when being pulled over irregular surfaces.

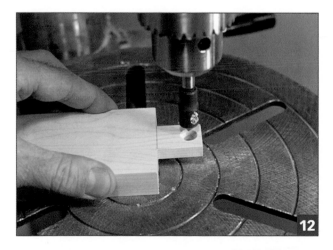

13. Cut a short length (⅞ in. long) of ¼-in.-dia. dowel for each car. Sand one end smooth, and slightly bevel the sharp corners on both ends.

14. Place a little glue in the ¼-in.-dia. hole in the smaller tab, and tap the dowel into place with the sanded end up. Make it even with the top of the frame and protruding out the bottom about ¹/₁₆ in.

15. When the glue is hard, sand the bottom end of the dowel flush with the car frame.

16. Sand the small bevels on the ends of the tabs. I find that a disk sander works best for this.

17. Bevel all sharp corners slightly, except for the long edges along the top of the frame.

Axle Housings

These housings are the same for all the cars; each car will need two. They are short blocks that are drilled for the axle pins, with other smaller blocks acting as spacers. Wheels are added only after the car is complete. Drill the holes before cutting the wood into blocks, because once the housings are cut, their small size makes them difficult to hold accurately in the drill press.

AXLE HOUSINGS

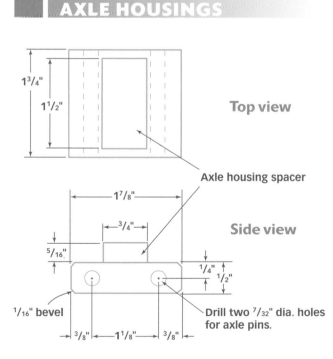

1. Cut a strip of wood 1¾ in. wide by ½ in. thick by at least 24 in. long (if you are making six cars). See the cut list on p. 105.

2. Lay out for the holes. It's best to lay out on both sides because the drill may wander a little, depending on the grain, coming out the bottom off center. Drilling carefully from each side eliminates this problem. The 1⅛-in. spacing can vary a little, but the holes should be very close to center.

3. Drill the holes using a drill press. Check that the housings are held square to the table. The standard axle pins I use require a ⁷⁄₃₂-in. drill.

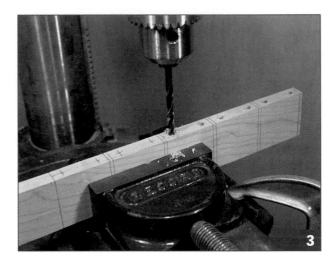

I find that it's best to leave the vise clamped in location, merely loosening it to move the wood along until the next hole is lined up, because it ensures quick and accurate centering.

4. Cut each housing 1¾ in. long.

5. Sand or file the ends square. I use a disk sander with a fine-grit wheel and a simple miter gauge that I made to keep the ends square to the disk.

6. Bevel all sharp corners slightly.

7. Cut out the spacer material (⁵⁄₁₆ in. thick by ¾ in. wide by 24 in. long). The easiest method is to saw ⁵⁄₁₆-in. slices of ¾-in.-thick wood.

8. Cut the spacers to length (1½ in.), and sand the ends smooth.

9. Glue the spacers to the axle-housing blocks. Center them each way.

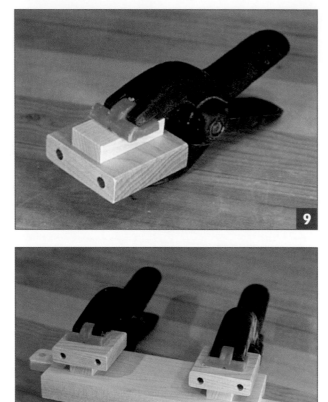

10. Glue the axle housings to the underside of the car frames. Check that they are centered sideways and square to the frame.

11. Remove the excess glue.

PART NAME	FINISH DIMENSIONS L X W X T	NO. REQ'D.
Box sides	5⅜ in. x 1¼ in. x ⅜ in.	2
Box front end	1 in. x 1⁹⁄₁₆ in. x ⅜ in.	1
Box back end	1¼ in. x 1⁹⁄₁₆ in. x ⅜ in.	1

Coal Tender

This car consists of a shallow box sized specifically to accommodate three cubes, six triangular half cubes, or some combination of cubes and triangles. Of course, kids can use it to haul rocks, small stuffed animals, or any number of things. The box is attached to one of the train-car frames made previously (see p. 104).

1. Cut a strip of ⅜-in.-thick (it could also be ½-in.) wood; for this project, I used purpleheart. This strip will form the bottom and ends of the box. It should be at least 2½ in. long by 1⅝ in. wide. The length and width are sized to give the blocks ⅛-in. clearance, allowing young children to load and unload easily.

2. Cut the ends to length, keeping the cuts square.

3. Lay out for the sides on a 1¼-in.-wide piece of ⅜-in.-thick wood (it could also be ¼ in. thick, as long as the inside dimensions of the box remain the same).

4. Saw the sides, leaving a little extra length for now (about ¹⁄₃₂ in. to ¹⁄₁₆ in. oversize).

5. Sand and shape the sides as needed, but don't worry about the end grain for now. This will be trimmed after assembly.

6. After all the inside surfaces are finish-sanded, assemble the parts dry. When you've established that all the parts fit accurately, glue and clamp them together. Keep edges flush on the top because it's easier to sand the bottom flush.

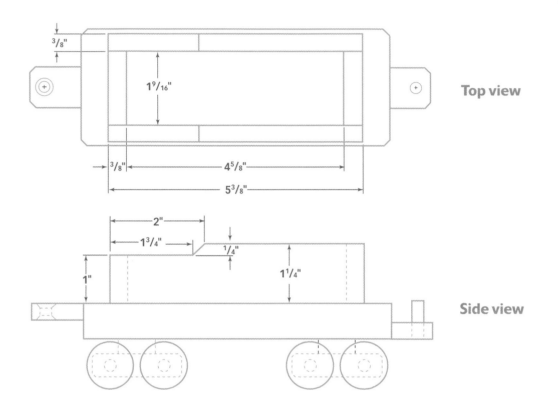

3/8"

1⁹/₁₆"

3/8" | 4⁵/₈"

5³/₈"

Top view

2"

1³/₄"

1/4"

1"

1¹/₄"

Side view

7. Plane and/or sand the bottom edges of the box flat and flush.

8. Sand all sharp corners around the top of the box.

9. Sand the car frame, removing all sharp corners.

10. Glue the box to the frame.

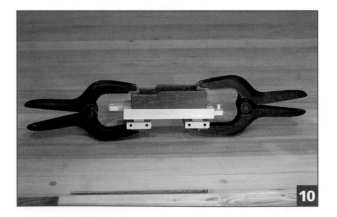

11. Put the wheels on the car, as you did for the locomotive (see p. 101, 102).

12. To make the cargo cubes and triangles, see the Ultimate Building Block Set (p. 72). The blocks that work best are the cubes (A-1), half cubes (triangles, H-2), or quarter cubes (small triangles, H-1). The car holds three cubes, six half cubes, or 12 quarter cubes, as well as various combinations of these three types of blocks. If you make all of these blocks (21 blocks total), you would have all possible combinations, although you may want to keep it simpler for young children.

FRACTION STACKER CAR CUT LIST

PART NAME	FINISH DIMENSIONS L X W X T	NO. REQ'D.
Dowel posts	½ in. dia. x 2¾ in.	4
Unit block	1½ in. dia. x 2 in.	1
Half blocks	1½ in. dia. x 1 in.	2
Third blocks	1½ in. dia. x ⁴³⁄₆₄ in.	3
Quarter blocks	1½ in. dia. x ½ in.	4

Fraction Stacker Car

This car consists of 10 cylindrical blocks that stack on four posts. The blocks are sized so that there is a full-length block, two half-length blocks, three one-third-length blocks, and four quarter-length blocks. You may use slightly smaller dowel for the posts and blocks if the larger sizes are not readily available to you.

1. Using one of the train-car frames made earlier (see p. 104), lay out the holes for the four posts.

2. Drill the holes, using a stop to keep them ½ in. deep. If your drill doesn't have a stop, lower the table to a height that keeps the drill from going too

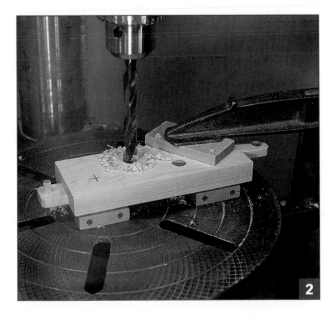

deep or mark the drill with a piece of tape. If the holes go deeper, or right through, adapt the length of the posts accordingly.

You may want to check that your drill bit produces a hole that fits the dowel snugly. Sometimes a drill cuts oversize, and the size of dowel varies. Better to check the fit on scrap wood first.

3. Cut four posts from ½-in.-dowel. They should protrude at least 2⅛ in. above the train-car deck after installation, so it's likely you will cut them 2⅝ in. long (unless you got a little carried away in the drilling process).

4. Sand the ends and bevel the corners. The top end should have a larger bevel (at least ¹⁄₁₆ in.).

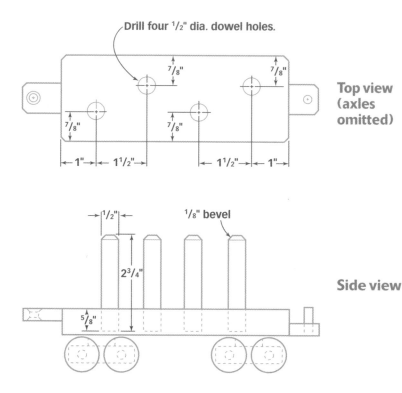

Drill four ¹/₂" dia. dowel holes.

Top view (axles omitted)

⁷/₈"   ⁷/₈"

⁷/₈"   ⁷/₈"

←1"→|←1¹/₂"→| |←1¹/₂"→|←1"→

Side view

→|¹/₂"|←   ¹/₈" bevel

2³/₄"

⁵/₈"

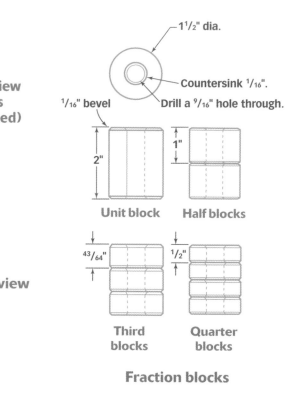

1¹/₂" dia.

Countersink ¹/₁₆".

¹/₁₆" bevel   Drill a ⁹/₁₆" hole through.

2"   1"

Unit block   Half blocks

⁴³/₆₄"   ¹/₂"

Third blocks   Quarter blocks

Fraction blocks

5. Put glue in the train-car holes using a toothpick. Install the dowels.

6. Put the wheels on, as you did for the locomotive and other cars (see p. 101).

7. Cut the dowel blocks to length. You will need about 9½ in. of 1½-in.-dia. dowel. Saw these pieces using a miter gauge and the bandsaw, and leave them ½ in. oversize to allow for some sanding later.

After each cut, sand the end of the dowel flat and square. It is much easier to square one end while the dowel is still long. This way the block will have only one sawcut surface needing sanding and squaring. You could file and sand this, but I tend to use a disk sander with a fine-grit wheel. A miter gauge is a big help here.

You want the two half blocks to add up to the same height as the large block (ideally within ¹/₆₄ in., definitely within ¹/₃₂ in.), the two quarter blocks to stack up to the same height as one half block, and so on.

8. After cutting, smooth the unsanded ends of each disk, either by hand or very carefully with a disk/belt sander. Check often that the disk ends are parallel to each other and square to the sides. Bevel the sharp corners slightly.

9. Lay out for the center on each block, which is where you'll drill the ⁹⁄₁₆-in.-dia. hole.

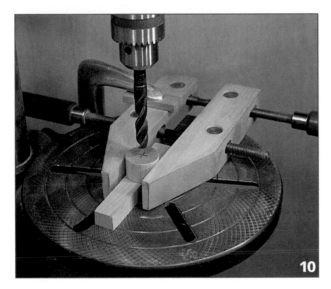

10. If you have a lathe with a three-jaw or four-jaw chuck, use it for drilling the center hole. Otherwise, clamp the blocks in a drill press. If you're using a vise, be careful when gripping the thinner blocks. The vise pressure can make the blocks a bit oval and crack them when the drill is breaking through, so use minimal clamping pressure.

11. Bevel the corners of the holes with sandpaper or with a countersink bit if you have one.

12. Install the wheels as you did with the locomotive (see p. 101).

Color Pattern Car

This car provides an opportunity for children to practice patterning, a premath skill. Up to nine layers of colored slabs can be used at once, so decide which and how many colors you want the slabs to be. It doesn't hurt to make a few extras, as it will lend variety to the play, allowing you to vary the difficulty level of the patterning. If you want the patterning to be kept simple, use only two or three colors of wood.

Hobby stores, some larger building-supply stores, and mail-order companies (like Lee Valley) carry short lengths of ¼-in.-thick wood in exotic species. You may also want to use only maple or other light-colored wood and then dye them. For this project, I ended up making a dozen slabs with four different-colored woods: yellowheart, purpleheart, maple, and padauk.

PART NAME	FINISH DIMENSIONS L X W X T	NO. REQ'D.	NOTES
Dowel posts	½ in. dia. x 3⅛ in.	2	
Colored slabs	4¾ in. x 2 in. x ¼ in.	8 or 12	Make two or three of each color. Use different types of wood, or light-colored wood with stain or dye.

1. Using one of the train-car frames made earlier (see p. 104), lay out the two post holes, 3 in. apart and on center sideways. I have used ½-in.-dia. dowel to keep the posts blunt and strong, suitable for young children.

2. Drill the holes, but do not drill right through. Stop with about 1/8 in. of wood remaining, just as you did in step 2 of the fraction stacker car (see p. 111).

3. Cut two dowel posts, 3⅛ in. long. Sand one end, and bevel the edges slightly.

4. Put glue in the holes using a toothpick, and tap the dowels into place.

5. Install the wheels as you did with the locomotive (see p. 101).

6. Cut the material for the slabs ¼ in. thick by 2 in. wide.

7. Cut slabs to 4¾-in. lengths. A table saw, miter saw, or bandsaw will work just fine. You will need at least 57 in. of total length if you are making 12 slabs, 43 in. if you are making only nine. It is nice to have the ends square and the lengths identical, but neither is critical.

8. Sand the ends smooth. Bevel all sharp corners.

9. After cutting the slabs to length, lay out one slab for the two holes. These holes should be spaced exactly the same as the holes on the train car, designed to be 3 in. apart.

10. Stack and clamp the slabs to the drill-press table, with a scrap piece underneath. Take your time to ensure that the pile is square on the sides, not leaning or irregular.

11. Drill the holes using a ⁹⁄₁₆-in. bit (it can be slightly larger if you don't have a ⁹⁄₁₆-in. bit). You want to have a decent amount of clearance so that the stacking activity is manageable for young children.

12. Sand all surfaces of the slabs, and bevel all the sharp corners. Use a countersink bit on the holes if you have a bit the appropriate size; otherwise, just sand the edges of the holes, as I did.

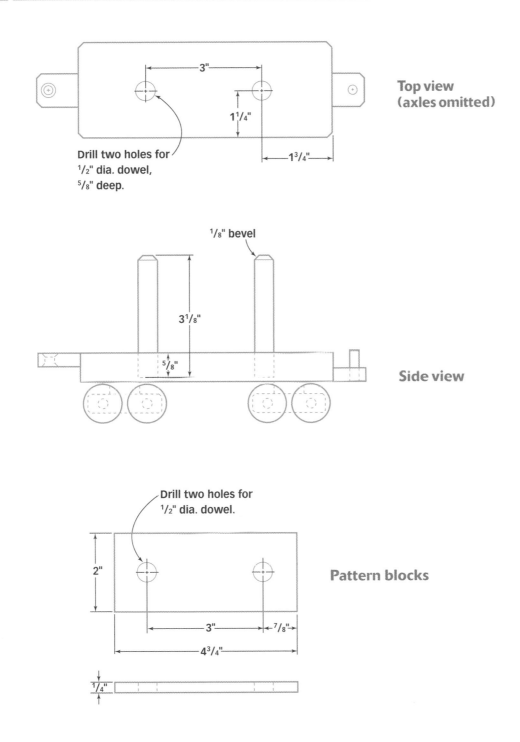

3"

1¹/₄"

1³/₄"

Drill two holes for
¹/₂" dia. dowel,
⁵/₈" deep.

**Top view
(axles omitted)**

¹/₈" bevel

3¹/₈"

⁵/₈"

Side view

Drill two holes for
¹/₂" dia. dowel.

2"

3"

⁷/₈"

4³/₄"

¹/₄"

Pattern blocks

PART NAME	FINISH DIMENSIONS L X W X T	NO. REQ'D.	NOTES
Deck	6½ in. x 2½ in. x ¾ in.	1	Thickness can be ½ in. or 1 in.
Cube	1½ in. x 1½ in. x 1½ in.	1	
Half cube	1½ in. x 1½ in. x 1½ in.	1	
Cylinder	1½ in. dia. x 1½ in.	1	

Geometry Puzzle Car

This simple puzzle car has three geometric shapes that fit into corresponding recesses in the car deck. Two of the blocks—the cube and the triangle—are directly out of the Ultimate Building Block Set (see p. 72). The other block is a cylinder made from a 1½-in.-long piece of 1½-in.-dia. dowel, the same size used for the fraction stacker car.

1. Cut the deck from ¾-in.-thick wood (½ in. to 1 in. would work as well) to 2½ in. wide by 6½ in. long. This is the same size as the train-car frame, without the couplers on the ends. Cut the length as close as possible, but leave the sides ½₂ in. oversize and finish them after assembly. To add color to this car, I used some of my remaining purpleheart.

2. Lay out for the three shape cutouts on the side that will be glued to the frame (the coping saw may cause some splitting). You can also ignore splinter and chipping problems until the deck is complete and then plane or sand down about ¹⁄₁₆ in., leaving a smooth surface.

3. Lay out for a ¼-in.-dia. hole in each corner of the square and triangular cutout, and lay out for one hole somewhere along the rim of the circle. The center of the holes will be ⅛ in. away from the cutouts' edges. These holes will allow you to insert the coping-saw blade. Locate the holes as accurately as possible.

4. Drill the ¼-in.-dia. holes.

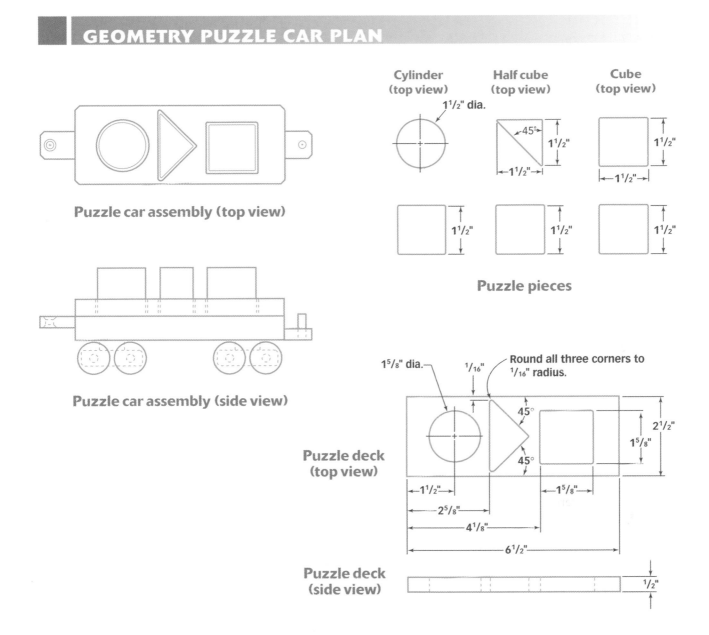

Puzzle car assembly (top view)

Puzzle car assembly (side view)

Cylinder (top view)

1¹⁄₂" dia.

Half cube (top view)

45°

1¹⁄₂"

1¹⁄₂"

Cube (top view)

1¹⁄₂"

1¹⁄₂"

1¹⁄₂"

1¹⁄₂"

1¹⁄₂"

1¹⁄₂"

Puzzle pieces

Puzzle deck (top view)

1⁵⁄₈" dia.

¹⁄₁₆"

Round all three corners to ¹⁄₁₆" radius.

45°

45°

2¹⁄₂"

1⁵⁄₈"

1¹⁄₂"

1⁵⁄₈"

2⁵⁄₈"

4¹⁄₈"

6¹⁄₂"

Puzzle deck (side view)

¹⁄₂"

5. To help ensure that the saw isn't cutting at an angle, lay out the shape on the reverse side of the deck. Simply joining the edges of the holes will provide a fairly accurate guide, assuming the holes are reasonably precise.

6. Saw out the shapes. The coping saw will tend to splinter the wood a little on the "top" side as the blade pulls through. If this does not suit your wood, you may want to saw from the opposite side so the best side ends up on top.

6

7. File and sand the cutouts. I start with a half-round file, then use my 6-in. double-cut smooth file, and sand a bit when I'm finished.

Also file or sand a small bevel on the edges of the top side.

8. Sand the top of one of the train-car frames made earlier (see p. 104). Use a sanding drum and drill press for the round hole (see photo #11 on p. 58).

9. Glue the deck to the train-car frame.

10. Plane and sand the edges flush.

11. Make the cube and the triangle following the instructions from the Ultimate Building Block Set (see p. 71).

12. Cut the 1½-in.-dia. dowel block, as you did with the fraction stacking blocks earlier in this chapter (see p. 112).

13. Sand to remove all sharp corners.

14. Install the wheels as you did with the locomotive (see p. 101).

Log Car

This car is always a favorite with kids, and it couldn't be easier to make. It simply consists of embedding dowel posts in the four corners of one of the train-car frames made earlier (see p. 104).

1. Lay out for the four holes on a car frame.

2. Drill holes to fit ⅜-in.-dia. dowel. Drill a sample hole in scrap wood just to make sure the dowel will fit reasonably snugly.

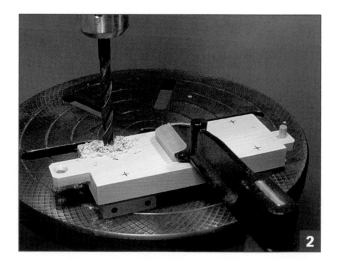

PART NAME	FINISH DIMENSIONS L X W X T	NO. REQ'D.	NOTES
Dowel posts	⅜ in. dia. x 2 in.	4	
Logs	½ in. dia. x 6 in.	9	Optional; could use short pieces of willow or other sticks.

3. Cut four, 2-in.-long pieces of ⅜-in.-dia. dowel.

4. Sand and bevel one end.

5. Use a toothpick to put glue in the holes and then tap the dowels in place.

6. Install the wheels as you did with the locomotive (see p. 101).

7. The logs for this car are simply dowels cut to length (⅝-in.-dia. dowel, cut about 6 in. long works well). I have also used 6-in. lengths of small branches from willow bushes, between ½ in. and ¾ in. in diameter. The latter are more realistic, but you have to go find some suitable shrub or tree.

LOG CAR PLAN

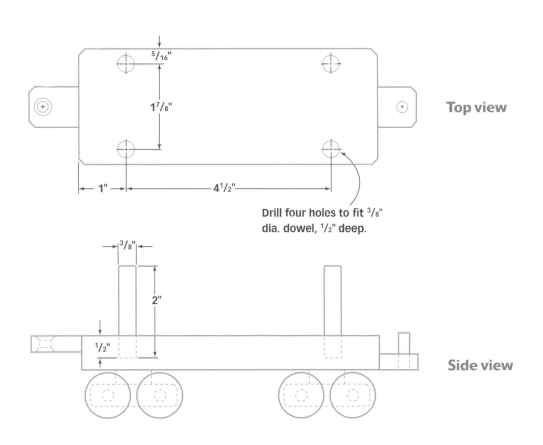

Top view

Drill four holes to fit ³/₈" dia. dowel, ¹/₂" deep.

Side view

Boxcar

The boxcar is just that—a box on a car. It has a side door for loading and unloading whatever cargo is used. The joints are simple butt joints, but they work well because the grain on the end pieces runs vertically, eliminating end-grain butt joints.

1. Cut the sides 2¼ in. wide by 6½ in. long by ¼ in. thick. These could be ¹⁄₆₄ in. to ¹⁄₃₂ in. oversize in length to allow for sanding of the ends after assembly.

2. Cut the end pieces 2 in. wide by 2¼ in. long by ⅜ in. to ¾ in. thick. I had ⅜-in.-thick wood, so I used it.

BOXCAR PLAN

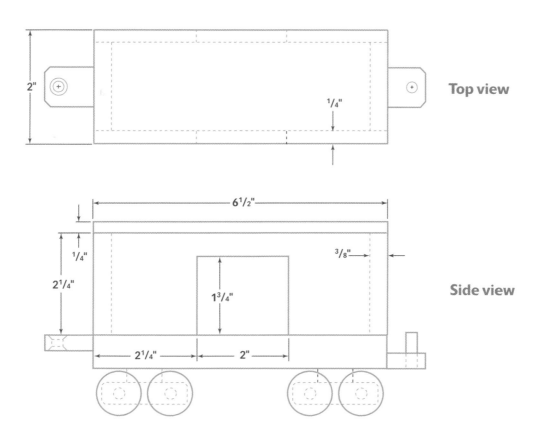

Top view

2"

1/4"

Side view

6¹/₂"

1/4"

2¹/₄"

3/8"

1³/₄"

2¹/₄"

2"

BOXCAR **CUT LIST**

PART NAME	FINISH DIMENSIONS L X W X T	NO. REQ'D.
Sides	6½ in. x 2¼ in. x ¼ in.	2
Ends	2¼ in. x 2 in. x ⅜ in.	2

3. Lay out for the door cutout on both sides of the 2¼-in. by 6½-in. pieces.

4. Saw the door cutouts. File and sand as needed, breaking all the sharp corners.

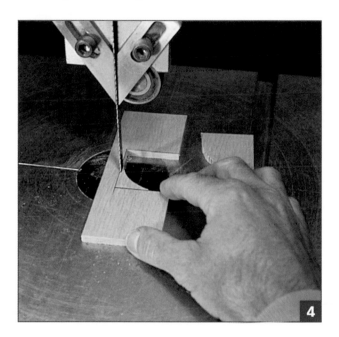

5. Sand the inside surfaces of the boxcar's sides and ends.

6. Assemble the box without glue so you can set up your clamps. Make sure the grain on the end pieces is running vertically to avoid gluing to end grain. Make sure the sides are even with the end

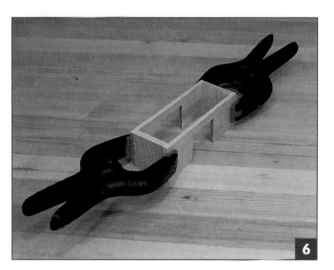

pieces or protruding past them slightly (¹⁄₆₄ in.). When everything works to your satisfaction, apply glue to the end pieces and clamp.

7. Sand to even all surfaces. Use a sanding board to sand the top and bottom of the box.

8. Make the roof of the car by tracing the box onto a piece of ¼-in.-thick wood. Make the roof slightly oversize so it just barely overlaps the box on all sides. Cut the roof.

9. Glue the roof to the box.

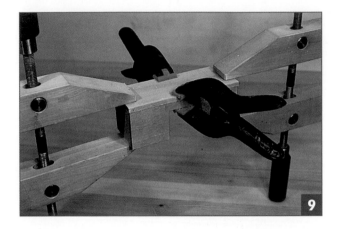

10. When the glue is hard, sand the box until all the surfaces are flush. It should sit flat on the car frame and should be even with the outsides of the frame when set on the frame.

11. Glue the box to the frame.

12. Install the wheels, as you did for the locomotive (see p. 101).

Caboose

The caboose, like the locomotive, makes the puzzle cars into a train. The body of the caboose is made much like the boxcar. The cupola (small raised-roof section) is just a block of wood hollowed out by drilling two large holes in it. The roof of the main part of the caboose has two similar large holes

PART NAME	FINISH DIMENSIONS L X W X T	NO. REQ'D.	NOTES
Sides	5½ in. x 1¾ in. x ⅜ in.	2	Could use ½ in. thick.
Caboose roof	6½ in. x 2¾ in. x ¼ in.	1	
Stack	¼ in. dia. x 1 in.	1	Cut 1¹⁄₁₆ in.; trim later.
Cupola	2⅜ in. x 1½ in. x ¾ in.	1	
Cupola roof	2½ in. x 1¾ in. x ¼ in.	1	Could be ⅛ in. thick.

drilled in it, so that you can see down into the caboose through the small porthole windows in the sides of the cupola. This ends up being important to the final appearance.

The windows in the caboose body, as well as in the cupola, are just drilled holes. The sides as well as the cupola are made from padauk, although any wood that has a dramatic color would work just as well. The roofs are maple.

1. Rip a ⅜-in.-thick board 1¾ in. wide. It will need to be at least 11¼ in. long because it will supply material for both sides of the caboose. Keep the edges parallel because both sides should have exactly the same width.

2. Cut the two side pieces to length. They will be 1¾ in. wide by 5½ in. long.

3. Sand the ends smooth and square. Bevel all sharp corners.

4. Lay out for the window holes on one side piece. See the drawing on p. 124 for hole locations.

5. Clamp both pieces on a drill press, preferably on a scrap piece to reduce splinters as the drill breaks through. Drill with a ¾-in. bit.

6. Break the sharp corners around the holes using a countersink bit or a small file and sandpaper.

7. Cut the caboose roof (6½ in. by 2¾ in.) from a piece of ¼-in.-thick wood. While you're at it, cut out the roof for the cupola (1¾ in. by 2½ in.).

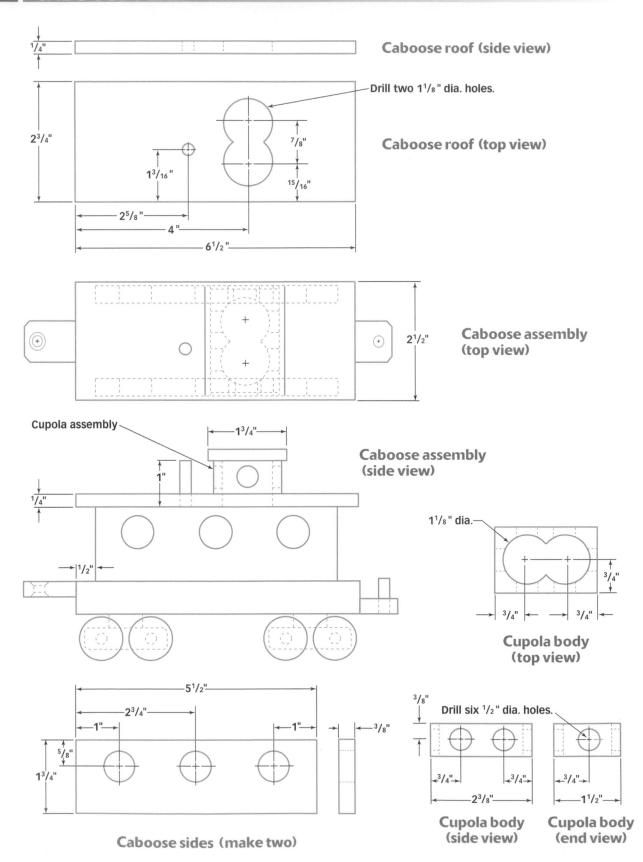

1/4"

Caboose roof (side view)

Drill two 1¹/₈" dia. holes.

Caboose roof (top view)

2³/₄"

7/8"

1³/₁₆"

15/₁₆"

2⁵/₈"

4"

6¹/₂"

Caboose assembly
(top view)

2¹/₂"

Cupola assembly

1³/₄"

Caboose assembly
(side view)

1"

1/4"

1¹/₈" dia.

1/2"

3/4"

3/4"   3/4"

Cupola body
(top view)

5¹/₂"

2³/₄"

1"   1"

5/8"

1³/₄"

3/8"

3/8"

Drill six 1/2" dia. holes.

3/4"   3/4"   3/4"

2³/₈"   1¹/₂"

Cupola body
(side view)

Cupola body
(end view)

Caboose sides (make two)

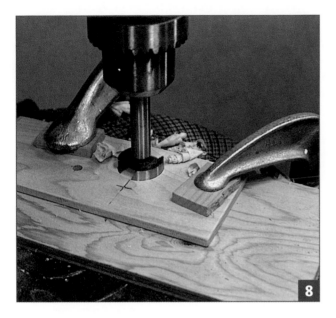

8. Lay out for the large (1⅛-in.-dia.) holes 4 in. from one end (see the drawing facing page). Drill using a Forstner-style bit, which allows the holes to overlap a little (you could use a small drill and a coping saw if no large bit is available).

9. Still working on the roof, drill the ¼-in.-dia. hole 2⅝ in. from the end. Again, you may need to drill a tiny bit oversize or sand the dowel a little, depending on the exact dowel diameter.

10. Cut the short piece of ¼-in.-dia. dowel for the stack.

11. Sand one end and bevel the corners slightly.

12. Glue the stack into the hole. Have the dowel protrude out the other side slightly.

13. Sand the dowel flush on the other side, once the glue is hard.

14. Assemble the sides, frame, and roof. When the setup works for you, apply glue and clamps.

Cupola

On old trains, some cabooses had the cupola in the center, some at the end. Kids tell me the end location looks better, so I put it there.

1. Cut a block of wood 1½ in. wide by 4 in. long by ¾ in. thick. It will eventually be cut to 2¼ in. long, but it is easier to clamp for drilling if it is left longer for now.

2. Lay out for the large (1⅛-in.-dia.) holes. The exact size of the cutout doesn't matter but should match the roof.

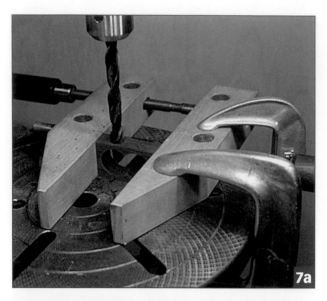

3. Drill the 1⅛-in.-dia. holes just as you did for the roof.

4. Cut the cupola to length (2¼ in.).

5. File and/or sand the ends square.

6. Lay out for the six ½-in.-dia. side holes (see the photo top right) and end holes (see the photo bottom right).

7. Clamp the cupola in a vise or with parallel clamps, and drill the side holes (see photo top right) and end holes (see the photo bottom right).

8. File or sand the sharp edges around the holes. A countersink bit could be used on the outside surfaces.

9. Sand all surfaces of the cupola.

10. Glue the cupola assembly to the caboose roof, lining up the cutouts as closely as possible. If the roof is flat and there are no gaps, clamping is optional.

11. Glue the cupola roof (cut out earlier with the caboose roof) to the cupola. Position it so that the overhang is even all around.

12. Attach the wheels, as you did with the loco-motive (see p. 101).

Finishing

For this project, I used two coats of Robson's Tried & True™ varnish oil on all the cars in this train, but a spray varathane or other plastic finish would work as well. See the introduction for additional finishing options (p. 13).

Learning through *Play*

THE PUZZLE TRAIN encourages creativity through open-ended play, as well as introducing math-based concepts. As a whole, it sharpens fine-motor skills and eye-hand coordination, while individual cars provide specific educational benefits.

The Coal Tender is a puzzle with many possible solutions that encourages problem solving, geometric relations, math skills, and imagination. It will hold several blocks of varying shapes from the Ultimate Building Block Set (described in the previous chapter), as well as any number of other objects.

When used in conjunction with the Ultimate Building Block Set, you can begin with young children by loading the coal tender with three cubes, then substituting one cube with two half cubes. Eventually use quarter cubes as well. You can also have children fill the tender using a certain number of blocks (3–12 are all options). Explain that two half cubes equal one whole cube. You could talk about numerators and denominators and how to write these fractions. A few short lessons tend to be better than one long one.

It is also beneficial to set the blocks aside, and see what type of load children can come up with. Have them describe their load, and tell why they chose those items.

The Pattern Car makes it easy to create and recognize simple patterns, providing a good foundation for later mathematics. It holds eight slabs of wood that are differentiated by color and/or shape (shape can be introduced by rounding the corners of some slabs), allowing a variety of stacked patterns to be made. You can make them simpler or more complex by choosing two, three, or four different colors of wood.

Children, especially young ones, simply enjoy open-ended play with this car, but it can also be used in a more purposeful manner. Stack the slabs and ask the child to find and describe the pattern. Then have the child create a pattern for you to find.

The Fraction Stacker Car offers the fun of stacking things up to haul them, but it also provides a clear illustration of the concept of fractions. Children can easily compare halves, thirds, quarters, and whole units, getting a clear picture of their relative size. They may be mixed and matched as well, allowing for the comparison of two quarter blocks to one half block, for example.

No matter how a child stacks the fraction blocks there will be opportunity to talk about the equivalent stacks. Show how four quarters (or fourths) make a pile as tall as one whole. Eventually ask questions such as: "Is two-thirds more or less than one-half?" To start, you may need to show how to stack the blocks to compare, but soon the basic concepts will become clear.

The Geometry Puzzle Car teaches shape recognition and comparison using three simple geometric shapes. Young children can simply place the blocks in the correct socket, while you explain the different shapes (a triangle has three sides, a square has four sides). This can eventually include descriptions of three-dimensional shapes with the cylinder and cube. As the child becomes more adept, the half cylinders in the Ultimate Building Block Set can be used in place of the circle block to introduce more complex geometric-shape relationships.

The Log Car and the Boxcar allow children to engage in open-ended play, as they load up pencils, toy animals, or blocks, fitting them all in as they use their creativity and imagination. Children can learn to describe their loads to you, and determine how well they work in this car. Talk to them about what types of limitations there are based on the car's composition (the size of the opening in the boxcar, for example). What kinds of things don't work well in the log car? (Marbles or sand.) What kinds of things are great? (Long straight things.) Whether or not the load falls off, learning takes place. Have fun with it.

The Caboose and the Locomotive are the traditional toy parts of the train. They make the various cars into a train, ensuring that the learning is fun.

sources

Wood Toy Parts, Dowel, Hardwood, Etc.

Atlas Dowel & Wood Products Co.
5819 Filview Circle
Cincinnati, OH 45248
(800) 541-0573
www.atlasdowel.com

Bear Woods Supply Co.
PO Box 275
Cornwallis, Nova Scotia
Canada B0S 1H0
(800) 565-5066
www.bearwood.com

Cherry Tree Toys, Inc.
408 S. Jefferson St.
PO Box 369
Belmont, OH 43718
(800) 848-4363
www.cherrytree-online.com

Constantines Wood Center
1040 E. Oakland Park Blvd.
Ft. Lauderdale, FL 33334
(954) 561-1716
www.constantines.com
Veneer and veneering supplies

Lee Valley Tools Ltd.
PO Box 1780
Ogdensburg, NY 13669
(800) 871-8158
www.leevalley.com

in Canada:
PO Box 6295, Station J
Ottawa, Ontario
Canada K2A 1T4
(800) 267-8767
Tools, wood, and wood parts

Stockade Wood & Craft Supply
785 Imperial Rd. North
Guelph, Ontario
Canada N1K 1X4
(800) 463-0920
www.stockade-supply.com
Wood and wood parts

Machinery and Tools

Woodcrafts and Supplies
405 E. Indiana St.
Oblong, IL 62449
(800) 255-1335
www.woodcraftssupplies.com
Distributor of Benny's Woodworks & Tools

Woodworker's Supply℠, Inc.
1108 N. Glenn Rd.
Casper, WY 82601
(800) 645-9292
woodworker.com
*Large dowels, General Finishes
Sealacell and Arm-R-Seal, hardware,
tools, and woodworking supplies*

Workshop Supply
PO Box 1060
100 Commissioner St. East
Embro, Ontario
Canada N0J 1J0
(800) 387-5716
www.workshopsupply.com

Amana Tool®
120 Carolyn Blvd.
Farmingdale, NY 11735
(800) 445-0077
www.amanatool.com

Bridgewood®
Wilke Machinery Co.
3230 N. Susquehanna Trail
York, PA 17402
(800) 235-2100
www.wilkemach.com

CMT® USA, Inc.
307-F Pomona Dr.
Greensboro, NC 27407
(888) 268-2487
www.cmtusa.com

Delta® Machinery
(800) 223-7278 (parts, technical assistance)
www.deltawoodworking.com

DeWalt® Industrial Tool Co.
701 E. Joppa Rd., TW425
Baltimore, MD 21286
(800) 433-9258
www.dewalt.com

Eagle Tools
2217 El Sol Ave.
Altadena, CA 91001
(626) 797-8262
www.eagle-tools.com

Enviro Safety Products
516 E. Modoc Ave.
Visalia, CA 93292
(800) 637-6606
www.envirosafetyproducts.com

Felder® USA
1851 Enterprise Blvd.
W. Sacramento, CA 95691
(800) 572-0061
www.felderusa.com

Freud® USA
6 Ledge Rock Way, #6
Acton, MA 01720
fax: (978) 635-1355
www.right-tool.com/freudpowtool.html
Sawblades

Garrett Wade Co., Inc.
161 Ave. of the Americas
New York, NY 10013
(800) 221-2942
www.garrettwade.com

General® International Mfg. Co. Ltd.
8360, du Champ-d'Eau
Montreal, Quebec
Canada H1P 1Y3
(514) 326-1161
www.general.ca

Grizzly® Industrial, Inc.
PO Box 3110
Bellingham, WA 98227
(800) 523-4777
www.grizzly.com

Guhdo®-USA, Inc.
1135 JVL Industrial Court Dr. NE
Marietta, GA 30066
(800) 544-8436
www.guhdo.com

Hammer USA
1851 Enterprise Blvd.
W. Sacramento, CA 95691
(800) 700-0071
www.hammerusa.com

Highland Hardware
1045 N. Highland Ave. NE
Atlanta, GA 30306
(800) 241-6748
www.tools-for-woodworking.com

HTC Products, Inc.
PO Box 839
Royal Oak, MI 48068
(248) 399-6185

Incra® Tools
Woodpeckers
(800) 752-0725
www.woodpeck.com

Jet Equipment & Tools®
PO Box 1937
Auburn, WA 98071
(800) 274-6848
www.jettools.com

Lab Safety Supply^{SM}

Lab Safety Supply℠
PO Box 1368
Janesville, WI 53546
(800) 356-0783
www.labsafety.com

Laguna Tools
17101 Murphy Ave.
Irvine, CA 92614
(800) 234-1976
www.lagunatools.com

Makita® USA
14930 Northam St.
La Mirada, CA 90638
(800) 462-5482
www.makitaope.com

Porter Cable® Corp.
4825 Hwy. 45 North
PO Box 2468
Jackson, TN 38302
(888) 848-5175
www.porter-cable.com

Powermatic®
619 Morrison St.
McMinnville, TN 37110
(800) 248 0144
www.powermatic.com

Ridgid®
Emerson Tool Co.
8100 W. Florissant
St. Louis, MO 63136
(800) 474-3443
www.ridgidwoodworking.com

Rockler Woodworking and Hardware℠
4365 Willow Dr.
Medina, MN 55340
(800) 279-4441
www.rockler.com

Rojek
7901 Industry Dr.
N. Little Rock, AR 72117
(501) 945-9393
www.tech-mark.com

Ryobi® Power Tools
1424 Pearman Dairy Rd.
Anderson, SC 29625
(800) 525-2579
www.ryobitools.com

Sears℠, Roebuck and Co.
3333 Beverly Rd.
Hoffman Estates, IL 60179
(800) 349-4358
www.sears.com

Shopsmith®, Inc.
6530 Poe Ave.
Dayton, OH 45414
(800) 762-7555
www.shopsmith.com

further reading

A to Z Teacher Stuff
atozteacherstuff.com/
Good articles on play as well as lesson suggestions

Block Play: Building a Child's Mind,
Early Years Are Learning Years; '97, no. 4 (August 3, 1997), NAEYC.
www.americatomorrow.com/naeyc/eyly9704.html.

Children's Foundation (CF) Child-Care Bulletin (April 1996): 3.
www. npin.org/pnews/pnew896/pnew896k.html

Choosing Good Toys for Young Children,
by S. Feeny and M. Magarick, *Young Children* 40, no. 1 (1984): 21–25.

The Creative Curriculum for Early Childhood,
by D. T. Dodge and L. Colker (Washington: Teaching Strategies, 1996).

Inventing Kindergarten, by Norman Brosterman (New York: Harry N. Abrams, Inc., 1997).

Kids/Blocks/Learning, by Patricia Gaffney Ansel, Yale-New Haven Teachers Institute (1997).
elsinore.cis.yale.edu/ynhti/curriculum/units/1993/1/93.01.01.x.html

Manipulatives: Tools for Active Learning,
by Barbara Backer, *Early Childhood News* (Nov./Dec. 1997).
www.earlychildhoodnews.com/archive/manipu.htm

A Parent's Guide to Imaginative Block Play: Why Blocks Are Still One of America's Favorite Toys
Available (free) from:
T. C. Timber
Habermaase Corp.
PO Box 42
Skaneateles, NY 13152
800-468-6873
www.tctimber.com

The Toy Manufacturers of America Guide to Toys and Play, rev. ed.
Available (free) from:
The American Toy Institute, Inc.
200 Fifth Ave., Suite 740
New York, NY 10010
General advice and good ideas on play and toys

What Should Young Children Be Learning?, by L. Katz, *Child-Care Information Exchange* 100 (Nov./Dec. 1994): 23–25.

Which Toy for Which Child: A Consumer's Guide for Selecting Suitable Toys, Ages Birth through Five and Ages Six through Twelve, by Barbara Goodson and Martha Bronson (1997).
Available from:
U.S. Consumer Product Safety Commission
Office of Information and Public Affairs
Washington, DC 20207

bibliography

Berk, Elaine. **"Hands-On Science: Using Manipulatives in the Classroom."** *Principal* 78, no. 4 (March 1999): 52–55, 57.

Carter, Beth. **"Master Builders: Move Over, Frank Lloyd Wright!"** *Arithmetic Teacher* 33, no. 1 (September 1985): 8–11.

Ernest, Patricia S. **"Evaluation of the Effectiveness and Implementation of a Math Manipulatives Project."** Paper presented at the annual meeting of the Mid-South Educational Research Association, Nashville, Tenn., November 9–11, 1994.

Gresham, Gina, Tina Sloan, and Beth Vinson. **"Reducing Mathematics Anxiety in Fourth Grade 'At-Risk' Students."** Research Report 143 (1997). ERIC Identifier: ED417931.

Rogowski, Gary. **"My Five Essential Power Tools."** *Fine Woodworking* 153 (Winter 2001/2002).

Werbizky, Lydia. **"Block Building: Its Role in Children's Learning as Seen by One Elementary School Teacher."** *Insights into Open Education* 24, no. 3. (November 1991).